Rock Art of Africa

Rock Art of Africa

Carson I. A. Ritchie

SOUTH BRUNSWICK AND NEW YORK: A. S. BARNES AND COMPANY

LONDON: THOMAS YOSELOFF LTD

PHILADELPHIA: THE ART ALLIANCE PRESS

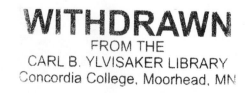

© 1979 by A. S. Barnes and Company, Inc.

A. S. Barnes and Co., Inc.
Cranbury, New Jersey 08512

Associated University Presses
Cranbury, New Jersey 08512

Thomas Yoseloff Ltd
Magdalen House
136-148 Tooley Street
London SE1 2TT, England

Library of Congress Cataloging in Publication Data

Ritchie, Carson I A
   Rock art of Africa.

   Includes bibliographical references.
   1. Rock paintings—Africa. 2. Africa—Antiquities.
I. Title.
N5310.5.A35R57 1977   759.01'1'096   76-24614
ISBN 0-498-01753-2 (Barnes)
ISBN 0-87982-024-1 (AAP)

Printed in the United States of America

For Jenia

Contents

Acknowledgments

I should like to express my thanks to the following individuals or institutions for the help that they gave me in preparing this book: Mrs. Stella Mayes Reed, my photographer, Mr. and Mrs. William Pawek, who lent me some of their photographs, Mrs. S. A. Bunyon, who also lent me photographs, Mr. Matola of the Malawi Tourist Board, the Rhodesian Ministry of Information, the Ministry of National Education, Tanzania, the South African Information Service, the British Museum, the Zambian Tourist Board, the Algerian Tourist Agency, the Tanzanian National Tourist Board, and many others.

Introduction

Though it is very difficult to know what constitutes great art, there can be no doubt that the rock paintings and engravings of Africa must fall into this category. Many people would feel that an art which had fulfilled its immediate purpose — that which exercised the makers of the rock pictures — but also retained enough residual force to captivate the people of today, people who are in almost every way a complete contrast to the rock painters would by so doing have demonstrated its power. Yet there must be many arts that are immediately attractive to the beholder without exercising one half the sway that rock paintings and engravings do over their votaries. What is there about rock art that makes it different from all the other arts of the world?

It is worth noticing that it is a secret art. The purposes for which it was undertaken, the motivation that inspired the artist in his often very difficult task, the techniques that he employed, his choice of subjects, the meaning of the symbols he employed, and the reasons why the art began, and then died out, all these are mysteries to us. There are only two statements we can safely make about African rock art: it is the most widely distributed of all art forms, and it is a school of painting that has been carried on longer than any other. These two bits of information are no consolation to those who would like to have the mysteries solved for them, and it is in an attempt to do just this, something that so many scholars and explorers have failed to do in the past, that I have begun to write this book. After all we are all human, and an unsolved mystery has claims on our imagina-

tion that no art that is a matter of record, where there is nothing to dispute, can ever have. Would we bother to look at the Mona Lisa if we knew what had made her smile?

It is good fences that make good horses. Just because rock art is an enigma, the African Sphinx that no Oedipus can interpret, it has attracted students of the highest order, men and women who have not hesitated to set their lives in jeopardy, making lonely desert journeys, or traveling through the wildest bush to add more listed rock sites to those we already know about. Less prominent, but certainly not less harrowing, have been the struggles made by scholars to solve the enigma. By comparison with hunting out rock shelters in snake- or leopard-infested bush, mere mental wrestling with a problem may seem a very small matter, yet there can be few fates more bleak than spending one's life looking for the answer to a problem that is never solved. Just because so many men and women of genius, integrity, and courage have searched for rock sites or submitted them to the scalpel of a keen intellect, the literature of rock art, though less than a hundred years of age, has attracted some of the brightest pages of the history of aesthetics.

Perhaps it is time we stopped talking about generalities and set out on a journey—a *safari* to use the local word, in search of just one painted site, one of the many thousands, that are to be found in Africa. The mere fact that we have to make a journey to this painted site lets us see just how different rock art is from the art of the present day. It is not

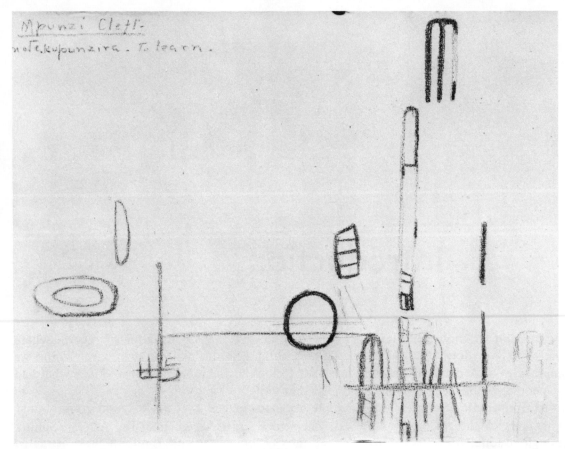

Another discoverer's drawing, from Mpunzi. (Courtesy of British Museum.)

The discovery of rock art goes on. Here, the distinguished archaeologist C.K. Cooke looks at a recently discovered painting. Since it shows riders on horseback, it cannot be more than 150 years old, the approximate date of the introduction of the horse to Rhodesia. (Courtesy of Rhodesian Ministry of Information.)

preserved in museums, or strong rooms, divorced from the life that gave it birth, with a curtain of glass, or even a bomb-proof stronghold, around it. Rock art has not been divorced from the life that gave it birth. It is still where it was created, in the painter's studio, which was also his living room, bedroom, and kitchen, a place where he made love as well as drew pictures, lived surrounded by his family and perhaps as we shall see, his fortress, where he made a last despairing stand against his enemies before he perished, and it became his tomb. Even after his death, imperishable aspects of the painter continue to be impressed on the walls of the rock shelter that was his studio and gallery. It is always a good idea to visit a painter and look at his work before it has left the studio, because it is only by trying to understand the painter that we can understand his work.

Little has changed in this painter's studio, a cave called "Mwalawolemba," a name that means just "Painted Rock" in Malawi, on Mikalongwe Hill, in the Southern Province, a district that, with South Africa and Rhodesia, constitutes one of the heartlands of rock art, the others being the Sahara, Rhodesia, and South Africa. The cave is just as it was,

Most painted caves are a palimpsest in which one set of paintings lies over another. The whole has to be disentangled and viewed as individual elements and not as a whole. (Photo Courtesy of Malawi Tourist Board.)

save that it has been swept out by the winds of heaven, the pictures are still exposed to the African sun, just as they have been for hundreds or thousands of years. During the wet season snakes take refuge in the cave, while at night the leopard rubs his spotted coat against the rough wall of the cave.

To get to Mwalamolemba, we have to take a very long ride from the capital of Malawi, Blantyre, followed by a shorter trip, but a much bumpier one, along an earth road without even a suggestion of road metal down the middle. The dirt road runs through fields of maize and bananas, and we stop before the

road does, because it is getting narrower and narrower and muddier and muddier, since it is the wet season. In this part of Africa, this does not mean that it rains all the time, but only that the clouds gather every day and it will probably rain once before evening.

As we trudge on, our forethought becomes apparent. A German tourist is also on his way to visit the cave and his Mercedes has stuck inextricably in the wet ground. Painted caves, even such remote ones as this, have become an object of pilgrimage to the art lover. Though as yet Africa's wild animals are more popular with the tourist than her art, this situation may change in the future and organized safaris, "tours of rock art," will begin. We would have liked to stop to talk to the German but he is obviously concerned about getting his car back on the road, no small matter in a country where you may have to

Rock paintings at Mphungi, Dedza, Malawi. (Photo
Courtesy Malawi Tourist Agency.)

spend the night sleeping under your vehicle for fear
of leopards until another motorist appears to give you
a tow.

The little African village at the foot of Mikalongwe
Hill appears deserted. Everyone is out in the fields,
but fortunately it is during the school holidays and,
besides the village, school, a converted tobacco barn,
with seats for the children made of piled up lumps of
dried earth, one of the school pupils appears—a very
friendly little girl called Mamma, who has profited by
her schooling and speaks excellent English. She brings
a girlfriend with her, also her brother, partly as a
chaperone, partly because he has got the family hoe,
so that he can go first along the path up the hill and
deal with any *njoka* (snakes) that we may meet.

The path is a very narrow slot that runs between
junglelike growths of elephant grass, much higher
than a man's head. From time to time an acacia
spreads its boughs across the path, and I instinctively
look up to see if any of the lianas that depend upon it
are, in fact, not vegetation but garter snakes. Then, I
look down again to the boulders at my feet because a
missionary friend, with whom I had been exploring
rock shelters on the headwaters of the Lengwe some
days before, has assured me that the gap between two
pieces of rock is *the* favorite place where snakes like
to hide.

It is a long climb up the hill, but Mamma and her
party take it at the usual breakneck speed with which
Africans move through the bush. From time to time,
they exchange comments in the tremendous voice
that is another African speciality and in which they
find it easy to communicate, even though one of
them is in one corner of a field and the other is in

14

A rock shelter, such as this Zambian example at Mkoma, did not merely offer a good painting surface. Its overhang protected the paintings (which are just visible in this example) from obliteration by rain during the wet season. Its shape may also have suggested the primeval cave, the womb from which both the animals and humanity emerged. (Photo Courtesy Zambian Tourist Board.)

another. We follow the now invisible children as best we can, reflecting that the noise that we are making will frighten away any leopards in the vicinity, while, as for snakes, at the speed at which we are traveling, we will have jumped over them before they are aware of us.

After what seems the longest climb in our lives, we emerge panting on the platform of a rock shelter on the side of the hill. A rock shelter is just what its name implies, the overhang of a cliff that forms an area of shade in sunlight and shelter in rain. Many rock shelters have what estate agents call a "favorable aspect." They look out on the direction opposite to

that in which the rain-bringing winds blow. It is very rare for painted caves to be particularly deep. A great depth of penetration into the rock would attract all sorts of unwanted fellow guests, of which snakes would probably be the least troublesome. Mamma points proudly to the symbols painted on the overhang of the roof, in natural earth colors of subdued red and white. Though pastel in tone, the colors look very fresh, as though the artist had left the painting only for a moment to go and get some more colors. The strange symbols on the roof include lines that emanate from a common source, then run in parallel lines. like a fountain. Others look like exclamation marks turned upside down, and many multiple dots made by dipping the finger in paint and pressing it against the walls of the cave. To touch one of these painted fingermarks, or the painted foot and hand imprints that occur in so many other cases, is to join hands with the Stone Age painter who made the frescoe possibly seven thousand years ago.

Though not the oldest art in the world, African rock art is certainly very old. Long before the first Pharaoh ascended his throne or the Israelites worshipped the golden calf in the desert, the rock artists were at work, and their ideas, infused into the circle of Neolithic civilization that ran from the Sahara to the shores of the Red Sea, may have influenced, in rather mysterious ways, all the great civilizations of antiquity. While the ancient Egyptians were certainly obsessed with some of the ideas of the cave painters,

These paintings in white from Mphungi, Dedzo, Malawi, may be more recent than the red formlings as white paint is not so long lasting as red. (Photo Courtesy Malawi Tourist Agency.)

These strange symbols are typical of the schematic art of Malawi. (Photo Courtesy Malawi Tourist Agency.)

Rock art may have been intended to be a "contact art" in which later viewers of the paintings touched them, thus receiving the vital life force that had inspired the original painters. (Photo Courtesy Malawian Tourist Board.)

These painting at Nqutu, Zululand, are hardly visible and require wetting from a nearby stream to make them show up. Though some authorities on cave painting feel that the paintings have not faded at all since they were discovered, others feel that processing with water and lemon juice by photographers, which allowed them to take better pictures, may have caused them to deteriorate. (Photo courtesy of South African Information Service.)

namely in creating paintings that would last forever, ancient Israel may also have come under the sway of the religion of cattle worship, around which so many of the Saharan paintings seem to center. What is stranger still perhaps is that the painters had not died out with the old civilizations. They had continued to paint right down to our own day, until the time when they had been wiped out by the Boers in their last stronghold, the Drakensburg, in South Africa, about a hundred years ago. The last of the cave painters had been a race called "Bushmen," people who had rather mysterious origins but who were decidedly un-African in that they were not black. Who the earlier cave painters had been was just one of the many mysteries that surround the art — *omnia exeunt in mysteria** might well, I reflected, be the motto of African rock art.

My attention was suddenly diverted from the very distant past to the immediate present by a feeling of indignation at the many modern names and drawings scrawled all round and sometimes over the paintings in the shelter.

*Everything ends in mystery.

While in many ways it was admirable that rock paintings should be open, informally to all, that they should not be enclosed in art galleries, or bought and sold, paintings that belonged to everyone belonged to no one. Iconoclasts, who disapproved of "pagan paintings;" art haters, art collectors determined to bring back painted slabs of rock for their country's museums, even if it meant dynamiting a whole painted site; visitors and photographers, who "freshened" the tone of the paintings by throwing water over them or rubbing them with half lemons; farmers digging for guano in the caves; herd boys who lit fires while they were sheltering from the rain; early pioneers who had used the painted animals for pistol practice; even cattle that had been penned in the caves and rubbed some of the paintings off the walls, all these and many more had contributed to the decline in the number of known rock paintings.

Archaeologists would sometimes list a painted cave, adding with fervent thanks the note that the particular site was so remote and difficult of access that it was unlikely to receive the visits of vandals. Many paintings had now been lost to us completely. They were only known to us from copies, copies that, though made meticulously and carefully, might have misinterpreted the intention of the original artist. My drawings had sometimes been redrawn by professional artists with numerous mistakes, so I felt it must be much easier to misinterpret a work that was thousands of years old, especially since the artists never painted on a completely flat canvas, but on the rugged contours of the cave wall. Some aspect of a drawing, such as the profile of a face, for example, which seemed to one observer to be a particularly happy stroke of the artist's imagination, might seem to another observer not to be in the picture at all, but to be merely a projecting knob of rock that somehow, through the viewer's imagination, had been worked into his interpretation of the picture.

What could be done to prevent the further vandalization of the paintings, I asked myself? The short answer to that was, "Nothing." It was impossible to close up the rock painting sites, as had been done in France, because they were not contained in deep caverns but in shallow openings in the face of the crags. When the most famous of all rock paintings, the *White Lady of the Brandberg,* was protected by iron railings, visitors who wanted to photograph it simply tore them aside. The South African government had lately undertaken a mammoth task that was

Many cave paintings, such as this schematic painting in Mpunzi, Malawi, are only known to us from drawings made by the discoverers, such as the one illustrated. (Courtesy of British Museum.)

in itself a counsel of despair with regard to rock art. This was to copy all the known paintings in the Republic and preserve the copies for posterity. Whereas Victorian amateur archaeologists like George William Stow had been content to go round the rock sites with a paintbox and pencil, together with wrapping paper when no better art paper was available, modern copyists used much more sophisticated methods. They laid photographic film, retaining the basic emulsion, on the rock and traced round it with a rapidograph pen. The photography of rock paintings had also improved enormously, so it was possible by looking at the art through both media, to get a good idea of what it was all about.

No copy, however perfect, could surpass the original, however, and the originals were fast disappearing. Or were they? Some observers refused to believe in paintings "fading" and said they were probably as fresh as when they were first copied. That did not apply to every painting. The *White Lady of the Brandberg* had become covered with a film of

mineral deposition because she had been soaked so often by photographers who wanted a nice sharp picture. She had also lost the most important attribute of a man − even a painted man − hence the dispute that had arisen about the sex of the portrait.

I reflected that it was a pity that some of the effort applied to photographing pictures that we could see had not been spent on photographing those which, though now invisible to the naked eye, probably still remained on the cave wall in the form of a deposit of mineral elements that would reflect infrared light and that consequently could be photographed in infrared. Attempts at this kind of photography had proved very successful in the Sahara, but little of the same sort seemed to have been done elsewhere in Africa. How interesting it would be to know for certain that the many rock shelters that seemed blank today had really not been painted in. And how much more interesting it would be if infrared photography revealed that they were full of unsuspected masterpieces!

Staring at the pictures on the wall, I tried to make sense of them, as so many had done before me. There is one great blessing for the art lover about rock paintings—no one is there to explain them to you. There are no guides or cicerones, while the available books on the subject are usually too heavy to be carried about. It is not considered necessary here, as it is in Zimbabwe, to walk round one of the greatest achievements of art wearing headphones and listening to a taperecorded account of what is to be seen.

Not that explanations are wanting. Students of the paintings have surmised that the dots on the wall may represent animals driven into an enclosure, or hunters within a *kraal,* while the parallel lines may represent that rain which is life to the Africans (if it had been a bad maize season, the fact would probably have appeared in the faces of Mamma and her brother — they would have been a lot less cheerful). The red and white lines that alternate in the paintings have been surmised to symbolize good and evil. They have the same significance to the modern Bantu. The symbols could be connected with the ritual scars inflicted on many African boys during their initiation into manhood. They could be cattle brands or the secret symbols used by members of a secret society such as one particular *vinyau* society that used to keep its costumes and masks in another Malawian cave. Possibly some of the symbols were those connected with sympathetic magic, and were designed to produce rain and good hunting. I knew from my study of Eskimo art that everything in engraving or sculpture

Cave painting from Kandanga, Tanzania, in late "white style." It depicts symbols that may represent animals in a game trap or houses in a kraal. (Photo Courtesy Ministry of National Education, Tanzania.)

had a meaning for the Eskimo. Even an apparently random collection of the lines and dots represented a seal, and therefore good hunting, and this was why the hunter scrimshawed the design on some part of his kayak gear.

Sympathetic magic, and a desire to secure good hunting had been put forward as an explanation for African rock art, too, not so much here in Malawi, where most of the paintings were schematic or abstract, but for the paintings of the rock galleries farther north and south, galleries that are a continuous frieze of animal paintings. There was no doubt that it was the animal paintings of the rock artists that had provided them with so many admirers. It was true that the schematic paintings were supremely satisfying, just as abstracts. You could enjoy them without knowing what they were about. Nonetheless, the animal paintings of the shelter artists had a special quality like that of the prehistoric cave painters of Europe. Wherein did this excellence lie? It was perhaps no accident that most people who came to Africa for any reason went to look at wild game, that they could see that the same game animals, rendered by artists who painted many thousands of years ago, gave them an added enjoyment in that they had seen the subjects and could compare them with the portraits. We cannot make the same comparison with a painting of a mammoth at Lascaux.

There was no doubt, too, that the rock painter knew his animals as few have been privileged to know them. It was not merely that he had followed their every movement so that he might dart an arrow at them, and could portray them in any aspect, browsing, fleeing, or making love (one painting in East Africa shows a female rhinoceros chasing a male, because, apparently, that is how rhinoceros courtships are carried on). Nor was it just that he had given the animal its due importance by eliminating the background completely (how fussy backgrounds have become in modern animal painting). He knew, of course, that it was the animal that you had to keep your eye on, because it was that which was liable to turn and rend you, not the tree in front of which the animal stood. The secret of the painter's success with animals lay rather in the feeling of mutual understanding that subsisted between them. The artist hunted to eat, but when he did kill, it was with a feeling of guilt, like that Cain felt about his brother's murder. "The game would not die, if we did not

Do these dots represent a hunting tally? (Photo Courtesy Rhodesian Ministry of Information.)

show respect for it,"[1] said an old Bushman. One of the ways in which the hunter showed his respect was by making paintings of his prey.

The old hunters, unlike some modern ones, had other stories to tell than those about animals. They had portrayed their battles, their journeys, some aspects of their religion. They had shown themselves among the sustained happiness of family life and the heady ecstasy of love. With what clarity and persistence of vision had the cave painters portrayed their destroyers, the enemies who were to drive them out, from, or exterminate them over almost the whole of Africa! Few of us would wish to paint the

portraits of our own executioners, but the cave painters of the Sahara had lovingly portrayed the arrival of the peoples of the sea in their chariots and armor, while the Hottentots, and Bushmen who are credited with some of the paintings of South Africa, had made lively sketches of the invading Bantu who were to supplant them.

I looked at the cave walls to see if they bore any signs of the final struggle in which many Bushman communities who lived and painted in caves must have been annihilated, struggles in which the little people were finally surrounded in their rock shelter homes by *impis* of the invading Bantu, and fell under a hail of assegais, still firing their poisoned arrows to the last. I had noticed that while some Africans showed a marked interest in cave sites, and were prepared to guide strangers to them, others dis-

[1] Francis Klingender, *Animals in art and thought* (Routledge Kegan Paul, London, 1971), p 18.

20

claimed any interest or knowledge about them. Was this because, to the African mind, the caves were still haunted by the vengeful ghosts of the Bush folk? Although we were in a part of Africa where the Bushmen had been exterminated before the whites ever arrived, I was not able to obtain any satisfaction from this historical fact. I knew that elsewhere in Africa, the Bushmen had been shot down "like baboons" by the whites. An English officer who was in Africa at the time of the Zulu wars, and whose reminiscence I had read just before I left home, remarked on the fact that having spotted a Bushman while he was out hunting, he decided he had better do the conventional thing and fire a rifle at him. However, being a mere visitor to the country and not a South African, he felt it was not really necessary to fire at the Bushman, so he discharged the shot well over his head. In South Africa, the Bushman, just before he laid aside his brush forever, used it to create lively portraits of his conquerors, the advancing

Hottentots, the Bantu warriors with their shields and bundle of spears, the Boers with their wagons and horses, and the British cavalrymen in their red coats.

The Bushmen, and their relatives the Hottentots, had been hated by black and white alike. Black people could see nothing in the little people to which they could relate, though they were, in fact, distant cousins of the Bushmen, and Bushman art contained many black elements, or supposedly black elements, such as ceremonial dancing by masked performers. The whites, too, found the Bushmen to be repulsive savages, though their cultural ancestors, the painters of the Sahara, had undoubtedly been partly Caucasoid. Rock art was neither white nor black, but a sort of cross between the Negro African and the white Mediterranean. As a mixed school, it had enjoyed not merely mongrel vigor but all the fascinating nuances of an art where continents meet. In this case, the continents had been Asia and Africa. From the East had come caucasoid and hamitic

The extermination of the Bushmen has posed a permanent problem concerning their painting. Here, they are being attacked by Bantu spearmen in a cave. From Wood. (Photo by Stella Mayes Reed.)

strains that had mingled with those of the negroid representatives of black Africa. The result had been a sort of universal art, of incredible width of scope as well as of outlook. West of where I stood, painted shelters stretched as far as the Congo and far northwest in Morocco. Eastward, they ran into Tanzania, Kenya, Ethiopia, and Somaliland. Northward rock art had filled the valley of the Nile, while it was only artistic convention that limited it to Africa.

If rock art was one of the farthest flung painting schools known, one that stretched right across a continent, it was also certainly one of the most productive ever recorded. How many painted caves were there? Thirty thousand had been discovered from the Sahara alone, of which about half were at Tassili. New discoveries were being made every day, but Africa was still a largely unexplored country, and it would not be surprising if, at the end of the count, those rock shelters that still remained to be found outnumbered those that were already known. Often, it was the merest chance that determined whether a painting site was brought to light or not. Mrs. D. R. Tweedie, an amateur archaeologist, had spent forty years searching the forests of Mount Elgon in Kenya, ignoring the buffalo and elephant that haunted them, before she found the painted shelter that now bears her name. The paintings on Lolui Island on Lake Victoria, which offer some rather unusual subjects, such as a canoe under sail, had been discovered only because police officers hunting Mau Mau terrorists had searched the shelter on the island in 1953. What was more, the probable total number of paintings was increased by the fact that many, if not most, African rock paintings were multiples. They had been painted not once, but again and again as new subjects were clapped on top of the old, till the whole frieze began to resemble a palimpsest, or document that has borne more than one written page of contents.

Composite picture of oxen and a lion, with a rhinoceros, two jackals, and figures that must be Bantu because of their spears. (Painting by Helen Tongue. Photo by Stella Mayes Reed.)

There is no virtue in the mere number of any kind of artistic representation, but the persistence of reproduction of the basic motifs or rock art, motifs that covered a dozen countries and as many millenia, is remarkable. Why had the rock painters been so determined to persist with just those motifs? Why had they painted the same spot again and again with overpaintings, when it would have been so much easier to scrub off the old painting with a sharp-edged stone and start again? They had shown plenty of patience in preparing an engraving, scratching or hammering it onto a smooth rock surface, pecking it out with sharp, pointed stones, and then, perhaps, polishing it. Yet, when they began to paint they were apparently seized with a mad desire to paint on top of another painting, one that had probably been painted by a previous artist. Why should this be so? For that matter, why should the painters want to paint at all?

No subject has been so thoroughly neglected by art historians as the psychology of the artist, particularly the primitive artist. Commentators on the paintings had obviously envisaged the Stone Age rock painter as a miraculously identical counterpart with the western painter of today. They had suggested that he painted, either for the sheer love of it, or to gain the admiration of his fellows, or in emulation to outdo the masterpieces of other painters. If those were not the right reasons, then he just painted to pass the time. Although I knew very little about primitive painting, my research into Malawian ivory carving had shown me that artistic talent was not something that one would lightly display in a primitive society, often it was much better to suppress it entirely. People with exceptional skill in any art had, quite recently, been regarded as bewitched, or even witches themselves. As for the suggestion that painting was merely intended to pass the time, I could not believe that anyone would travel through lion-infested country, making the journeys necessary to collect paintbrushes, pigments, and binding materials (all of which could not be found on any painted site) just to pass away an idle hour.

Yet, if the paintings had not been undertaken merely through a desire to paint, or, as one commentator put it, as a sort of Royal Academy in which those artists who had made a successful debut on skins or bark left their best work permanently on record on the stone walls of caves, why had they been painted? No one had, as yet, given a satisfactory answer to this fascinating problem, yet perhaps the solution to the problem of motivation might help to solve at least some of the other problems with which rock art was rife.

The long journey back from Mwalamolemba helped me to arrange my ideas on the subject more concisely. Part of the problem, I now resolved, was the fact that the approach to the whole subject had been too piecemeal. The rock art itself was incredibly wide in scope, both in time and geographical extension. At one end of the time scale, the artists had been in touch with the ancient civilizations of the Mediterranean. At the other, they had been exterminated by black and white invaders of Africa, the last of them disappearing less than a hundred years ago. Commentators on the paintings and engravings had tried to approach the art from one or other of its poles. They had come to the study of the rock galleries primed with a background to the classical period of North Africa, or their studies had been thoroughly rooted in near contemporary anthropology. Paradoxically, the earlier travelers in Africa, men who had a classical background but were also in touch with primitive Africans, had been in some ways better prepared to comment on the rock paintings than those of today. More than one early traveler, surely, had pointed out that the Bushmen strangely resembled the tribes of Ethiopia described by Strabo, tribesmen who wear arrows in their hair and can run faster then the wind.

What was needed was that someone aware of the discoveries in both North and South Africa, aware too that African art existed away from the continent of Africa—what writer, hitherto had attempted to include the rock engraving of the Canaries in an examination of rock art?—should try to make a *gestalt* of everything that was known of the subject. Such an attempt would, I knew, be unlikely to win favor from either northern or southern Africanists. When great scholars like Dr. Leo Frobenius or the Abbé Breuil had tried to synthesize the lessons of north and south, they had been treated with a certain coldness. People had said that they appeared to dispose of very considerable funds or that their researches were rather hurried. When they did try to step outside the limits of current orthodoxy, and to suggest, for example, that African rock art provided contacts with other continents, these scholars were regarded as cranks and told that African rock art was the painting of Africans by Africans.

The affair of the *White Lady of the Brandberg*, was a case in point. In a rock shelter of the Brandberg

Mountains in South Africa is depicted the running figure of a young person carrying a bow in one hand, and an enigmatic object in the other. The object carried may indeed be a cup or a flower, as has been surmised, but it bears some resemblance to the conventional symbol representing the outpouring of a man's seed on the ground. The figure appears to have long red hair tied up in a snood, but this may be a wig, because of what appears to be a white chin strap passing under the chin, perhaps to keep the wig in place. The figure is either dark skinned and partly painted white, or the other way round. The face color appears quite light in tone. Either white painted ornaments or rows of beads decorate the body. The figure wears shoes or, perhaps, just anklets that look like the tops of shoes. Tucked into a band passed round the right arm are two strange-looking implements. Apparently, the person portrayed is wearing shorts. So, at least, one commentator has said.

Reinhaart Maack, the archaeologist who first sketched the figure, drew it with a male member protruding, or at least (for we have only his sketch to go on) with something pushing forward that might be a genital sheath. The continuous drenching of the figure by photographers eager to secure a good print by heightening the effect of the colors with water has obscured this part of the picture, which, apparently has been coated by a semitransparent mineral deposit. The most extraordinary part of the picture yet remains to be described, however. Across the spot where the virile member would have been, if it were observable, is placed a transverse bar. This bar, say the Rudners and other Africanists, indicates infibulation. Infibulation was, according to the Rudners, carried out by the Romans to slaves and other to prevent them from having intercourse by sticking a "fibula bone needle" through the foreskin at right angles to the penis.[2]

The Rudners, while admitting that infibulation does not seem to be recorded in Africa otherwise than in the paintings, suggest that it was applied to youths in their initiation period or to men whom custom or circumstance prohibited from having intercourse with their wives. In fact, infibulation, as practiced by the Romans, seems to have been very different from what is conjectured by the Rudners or what appears to be portrayed in the picture. Samuel Pitiscus, the great eighteenth-century authority on

These human figures from a cave in Tanzania have a bar across them. Does this represent the taboo sign that occasionally crosses the members of the males in some pictures? (Courtesy of the Ministry of National Education, Tanzania.)

everything Roman, described "the gymnastic, or theatrical clasp *(fibula)*" which was attached to singers and actors so that their virile members were constrained, in order to conserve their voices and so that they were prohibited from the act of love,"[3] as "a ring or circle of bronze or silver by which the skin was pierced, closing that part which they did not wish to be exercised. It did not indeed, as is falsely believed by some, transfix the whole member, by which we are begotten, but only the cover of the glans of the penis." This was apparently what the Rudners believe infibulation to be, and they refer elsewhere to this attachment as "a long stick or bone point perforating the penis or foreskin at right angles."[4]

Such an attachment would be unwieldy in the extreme for moving through the bush, and it is significant that Breuil regarded it as an artistic expression of a sexual taboo. In the case of the White Lady, he apparently did not notice it, and it is noteworthy that one of the Lady's companions, who

[2] Jalmar and Ione Rudner, *The Hunter and His Art* (C. Struik, Cape Town, 1970), p. 57.

[3] Samuel Pitiscus, *Lexicon Antiquitatum Romanarum,* Leovardiae. Franciscus Halma, 1713. Vol. I. p. 777.

[4] Rudners, p. 198.

is apparently female, since she has been portrayed with breasts, also has this transverse bar.

The Abbé felt that the figure was that of a white girl, with a Mediterranean, probably Cretan profile, and with supple, youthful, and serene beauty. This identification was sufficient to draw on Breuil the onslaught of a whole commando of Africanists. C. K. Cooke and Alexander R. Willcox re-examined the figure and drew attention to the original sketch of the rock painting by Reinhaart Maack. While Willcox admitted the delicacy of the figure, he felt it had the grace of a boy rather than that of a woman. The figure, they decided, was undoubtedly male, partly because of the evidence of a genital sheath protruding past the thigh in the original sketch recording of it, partly because it was carrying a bow. Though both Lowe and Willcox felt that the Lady and her companions looked strange, neither were prepared to accept a Mediterranean origin for them.

At the opposite pole of rock painting, Yolande Tschudi had already encountered an almost identical problem, and tackled it in quite a different way. Speaking of the rock paintings of Tassili she remarks: "The sinuous line of the body could also make us imagine that we have to do here with a woman, a conclusion that would not be incompatible with the presence of a genital sheath, since the ancient history of Libya, for example, tells us that female sovereigns liked to adorn themselves with such an object, which was the symbol of power."[5]

When we read, subsequently, in Mlle. Tschudi's book that some Cyrenaican women were Amazons who fought in battle with men and follow her description of one such woman warrior who was beheaded by Theron and precipitated from her chariot at the battle of Saguntum, where she was serving as a mercenary with Hannibal,[6] it becomes less and less final that the White Lady was male just because she wore a codpiece (women have constantly assumed the attributes of the male sex throughout history, as all readers of Casanova know) or because she carried a bow and arrow. She wears the beading or white paint, and the ornamented snood worn by so many of the figures in the Tassili paintings, of whom a recent visitor to Tassili, Frank Elgar, has remarked: "We do not know whether we are in the presence of men, or women."[7]

Enough has been said to indicate the partial approach of many Africanists to this problem, an approach that has been one of my principal reasons for writing this book. Other reasons, however, are equally important. Rock art is much more widely known on the continent that originated it, and in Europe, than it is in America, where those who have heard of it have not perhaps grasped its real purport.

African rock paintings are not merely a blend of the white and black strains in history, something that Americans of all races can therefore relate to, they are also an astonishing mixture of traditional and modern art. It may seem strange to talk of an art as being modern when some of it is more than ten thousand years old, but the illustrations will speak for themselves. Many of the schematic paintings will probably prove much more acceptable as abstracts to lovers of contemporary art than the abstracts of today. The representational paintings of animals will also find their admirers. What about the portraits of humans? As will be seen from the account of the White Lady, the rock artists suffered from a vice that besets many portrait painters, even today. Nobody knows whom their portraits represent. This very defect, however, is a virtue in that it infuses into the whole story of rock art that element of bafflement without which the study of an art cannot be wholly satisfying intellectually, no matter what may be its aesthetic appeal. Let me hope that even if the reader does not agree with my conclusions, he will feel that the journey has been worthwhile.

[5] Yolande Tschudi, *Peintures Rupestres Du Tassili-N-Ajjer* (Neuchatel, Switzerland: A La Baconniere, 1956), p. 30.

[6] Ibid, p. 23. This incident has received literary expression in Vicente Blasco Ibanez novel *Sonnica.*

[7] Jean Dominique Lajoux, *Merveilles Du Tassili-N-Ajjer* (Paris: Editions du Chene, 1962), p. 134.

"Have you not hunted and heard his cry, when the elands suddenly start and run to his call?"

1

The Discovery of Rock Art

It is paradoxical that the rock art of Africa should have attracted attention long before that of Europe. It was not until 1878 that the daughter of the Spanish archaeologist de Santuola, who had gone with her father into a cave which he was exploring, pointed to the ceiling and uttered the famous words, "Look Daddy, bulls!" The famous frescoes of animals painted by Aurignacian artists now became known for the first time. Long before this, however, George William Stow had begun his careful copies of the Bushman paintings, while in the Canaries, and Africa, interest had already turned to the riches of the Stone Age—riches that were still being added to by the surviving painters, the Bushmen.

It was no accident that the painted and engraved art of Africa had come to light before that of Europe. In the first place, as has already been noticed, most of the rock art of Africa was surface art. It existed in rock shelters that were only skin deep compared with the deep caves of Europe. Furthermore, for those of an antiquarian turn of mind in Africa, there was little to do to assuage that European hunger for the past that is such a feature of the western outlook, except to explore for relics of remote times in African history. There was very little African art that could be collected, there were no documents, except in the north, though there was plenty of folklore.

The era of discovery of rock art started in Mozambique, where as early as 1721 paintings of animals were discovered by a Portuguese missionary who reported his discovery to the Royal Academy of History at Lisbon. Quite independently of the Portuguese settlers in Africa, the Dutch were beginning to explore their treasures. In 1752, an expedition led by Ensign August Frederick Beutler found many rock paintings along the Fish River of the Eastern Cape. These they attributed to the Bushmen. Johannes Schumacher copied rock paintings in the south or west area of the Cape around 1776 on an expedition led by H. Swellenberg, the governor's son.

More copies of paintings were made by another expedition, led by Governor Joachim von Pletterberg, which explored the Sneeuwbergen, or "Snowy Mountains" in the Eastern Cape district north of Graaf Reinet. The copyist may have been a certain Captain Robert Jacob Gordon—there was a whole regiment of Scots in Dutch service at this time, and this may help to explain the anomaly of a Dutch officer with a Scotish name. Most of Gordon's copies still remain, unpublished, in the Rijks Museum in Amsterdam.

Another expedition, that led by Grosvenor, from 1790 to 1791, found more Bushman paintings. Jacob van Reenen, who accompanied the expedition, noted in his diary that the explorers "reached the country of the Bushmen at a little thorn river, where on a rocky cliff the Bushmen had made a great many paintings or representations of wildebeeste, very natural, and also of a soldier with a grenadier's cap."[1]

Sparse references now begin to be made to rock paintings in travel journals kept by European explorers who were drawn to the marvels of South Africa. The two Swedish travelers Andrew Sparman and H.J. Wikar, who traveled independently of one another in South Africa in the 1770s, comment on paintings that they saw or heard of. One passage from the French traveler Le Vaillant's book on South Africa is particularly noteworthy. Le Vaillant, who was very much in touch with the Bushmen and who had happier experiences with them than any other traveler, except perhaps Gordon Cumming, nonetheless dismisses the Bushman paintings as "caricatures." He has, however, this to say about their purpose, speaking of the pictures in a cave of the Eastern Cape. "The Dutchmen believe them to be a century or two old and allege that the Bushmen worship them, but though it is quite possible, there is no evidence to show it."[2]

In 1797, Sir John Barrow made a journey into the interior of Cape Colony. After leaving Graaf Reinet, he tells us, "We made an excursion into the mountains on our left in search of Bosjemans" [the Boer word for "Bushmen"] .... The Kloofs and chasms leave a succession of caverns.... In one of these retreats were discovered their recent traces. The fires were scarcely extinguished, and the grass on which they had slept was not yet withered. On the smooth sides of the cavern were drawings of several animals that had been made from time to time by these savages.... In the course of travelling I had frequently heard the peasantry mention the drawings in the mountains behind the Sneuwberg made by the Bosjemans.... Some of the drawings were known to be new, but many of them had been remembered from the first settlement of this part of the colony."

Sir John made history by publishing (in black and white) a Bushman drawing. It was an animal's head that the author felt represented a unicorn. About thirty years later, in 1837 Sir James Alexander became the first to reproduce rock paintings in color, in a book called *A Narrative of Exploration among the Colonies of Western Africa*. They were taken from painted sites near Oudtshoorn, and the author

described the subject of the pictures he saw there as "a flock of sheep with their lambs represented in red ochre."

All these paintings were assumed to be the work of Bushmen, and to be near contemporary works. Obviously, many of them were. Sheep were a comparatively new importation to the Cape (we do not know whether they were long-tailed Syrian sheep, that could have been a lot older, or the European variety). The picture of a grenadier was, again, contemporary with the explorers who recorded it.

The Stone Age had not been formulated as a concept yet, so it is not surprising that no traveler had any inkling of the astonishing age of some of the paintings. Until comparatively recently, some writers persisted in asserting that they must all be the work of the Bushmen and that none of them could be more than a few hundred years old.

More than one traveler, however, was very critical of the artistic attainments of the Bushmen. Le Vaillant, who was nonetheless their great friend and admirer, has been already mentioned as a critic of their work. It may be presumed that he actually saw them painting, so that he could compare their contemporary work with what he saw in the paintings.

Thomas Baines, the famous painter of South African life, who has left us a picture of Bushmen artists at work, and who mentions rock paintings several times in his notebooks and diaries of the 1840s, includes "unicorns" and hunting and battle scenes, with men on horseback, in his descriptions. He too, like other artist travelers, such as Le Vaillant, is more than a little critical. Reverend J. G. Wood, who knew him well and was able to make use of many of his sketches for his book, quotes what is no doubt an opinion derived from Baines when he says:

"He [the Bushman] never fails to give the animals that he draws the proper complement of members. Like a child, he will place the horns and ears half way down the neck, and distribute the legs impartially along the body, but he knows nothing of perspective, and has not the least idea of foreshortening, or of concealing one limb behind another, as it would appear to the eye."[3]

A comment such as this, revealing that the Bushmen were ignorant of foreshortening, helps to throw doubt on their authorship of the paintings or rock

[1] J. and I. Rudner, *The Hunter and His Art*, p. 245.
[2] Ibid, p. 247.

[3] J. G. Wood, *The Natural History of Man* (London: George Routledge and Sons, 1875), I: 76.

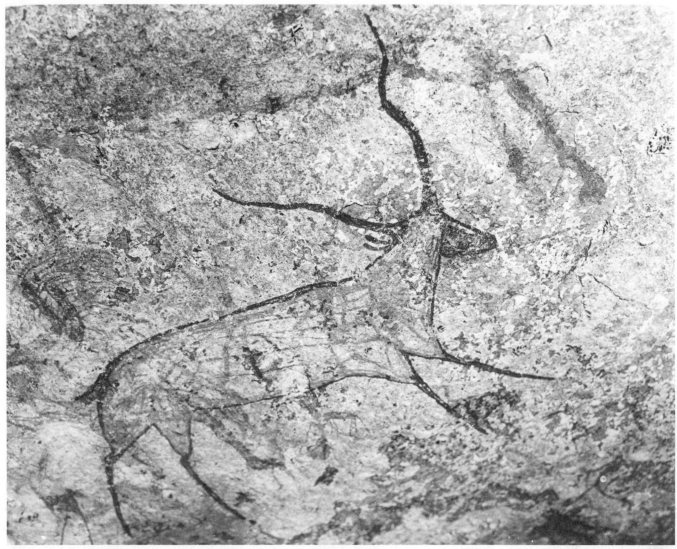

The placing of the ears behind the horns of this beautifully spirited antelope shows the liberties that painters were prepared to take with realism. From the Charewa Cave in Rhodesia. (Courtesy Rhodesian Ministry of Information.)

engravings that *do* display foreshortening. It was interesting to note what the reaction of the Bushmen was when Baines showed them one of his paintings. He found that they could understand a colored drawing perfectly, and name any tree, bird, animal, or insect that had been drawn in colors, but that they did not seem to appreciate a perspective drawing in black and white. "When I showed them the oil-painting of the Damara family," he wrote, "their admiration knew no bounds. The forms, dress, and ornaments of the figures were freely commented on, and the distinctive characteristics between them and the group of Bushmen pointed out. The dead bird was called by its name, and, what I hardly expected, even the bits of wheel and fore part of the wagon were no difficulty to them. They enjoyed the sketch of Kobis greatly, and pointed out the figures in the group of men, horses and oxen very readily. Leaves and flowers they had no difficulty with, and the only thing they failed in was the root of the markwhal. . . . The dead animals drawn in perspective and fore-shortened were also named as fast as I produced them, except a half-finished *uncolored* sketch of the brindled gnoo. They had an idea of its proper name, but said they, 'We can see only one horn, and it may be a rhinoceros or a wild boar.' "[4] Once again this passage raises problems. If the Bushmen could not interpret a realistic painting correctly, could their accuracy be relied on when they interpreted a

[4]Ibid, p. 77.

29

mythological painting, of the kind which George William Stow submitted to them? If they could not understand a simple black and white sketch, how could they have evolved monochrome paintings, as many observers were convinced that they had, before passing on to polychromes?

Another of Wood's informants, who was also an artist traveler, Mr. Christie, made further statements to Wood that may give us pause when we consider the Bushman's aesthetic abilities — abilities that were nevertheless then supposed to have originated rock painting.

"I cannot add much to what is written of them," he told Wood, "except to allude to what are termed Bushman paintings, found on caverns and on flat stone surfaces near some of their permanent water supplies. I have only met with two instances of the former paintings, and they were in a cave in the side of a krantz in the north part of the Zwart Ruggens. I came upon them while hunting koodoos.

"One side of the cavern was covered with outlines of animals. Only the upper part was distinguishable, and evidently represented the wildebeest, or gnoo, the koodoo, quagga, etc. The figures were very rudely drawn, and the colors used were dull red and black, and perhaps white; the latter may possibly have been a stalactite deposit from water.

"The other instance was near an outspan place on the Karroo road to Graff Reinet, known as Pickle Fountain, where there is a permanent spring of fresh water, near the course of an ancient stream now dry. On a flat piece of sandstone, which had once formed part of the bank of the stream, were the remains of a drawing, which may have been the outline of a man with a bow and arrow, and a dog, but it was so weather worn that little more could be made out than the fact of its being a drawing. The colors used, as in the cave, were red and black.

"At the time of my seeing the drawings, I had with me a Bushman, named Booy, who was born near what is marked in the map as the Commissioners' Salt Pan, but he could give me no information on the subject of the paintings, and I am rather inclined to think that they are the work of one of the Hottentot tribes now extinct.

"My Bushman was a very shrewd fellow, but, although I had been at that time for some years among the natives, I had not become aware of the poverty of their intellect. I had shown them drawings numberless times, had described them, and listened to their remarks, but had not then discovered that even the most intelligent had no idea of a picture beyond a simple outline. They cannot understand the possibility of perspective, nor how a curved surface can be shown on a flat sheet of paper."[5]

Christie sent Wood a copy of a drawing that he had discovered in a cavern in the George district. "The subject of the drawing," he told him, "is rather obscure. The figures are evidently intended to represent men, but they are unarmed, and present the peculiarity of wearing headdresses, such as are not used by any of the tribes with whom the Bosjemans could have come in contact. They might often have seen the Kaffirs, with their war ornaments of feathers, and the Hottentots, with their rude skin caps, but no South African tribe wears a headdress which could in any way be identified with those which are represented in the drawing."

Christie had thus raised to his friend Wood the two great difficulties that were to baffle later interpreters of the paintings. One was, as has been noticed, that the Bushmen were not completely trustworthy guides to what was considered to be their very own art. If all the rock paintings had been made by Bushmen, why was it that some could make no guess as to what they were all about, while others were only too voluble? Had the Bushmen completely forgotten their artistic traditions because of the changes brought about by the arrival of the whites or were the paintings the work of an esoteric, initiated, inner circle of painters? This was the position, more or less, that Stow was later to adopt, that Bushmen paintings were the work of "professionals."

The other problem was even more baffling. Why did "un-African" elements appear in various paintings? Were these merely due to bad drawing, or were they the work of some other non-Bushman folk? Had southern and central African been the forbidden land that it is often felt to be by Africanists, or had it been visited by exotic folk from the East? Like the headdresses of the men portrayed in Christie's shelter, the shorts worn by the White Lady are a case in point. So far as I know, only one other African is portrayed wearing shorts, a figure in an eighth-century Phoenician ivory found at Nimrud, a figure, significantly, of an African Negro, who is being savaged by a lion.

As the nineteenth century wore on, discoveries swelled the known total of rock drawings, but did not

[5]Ibid.

J.G. Wood's friend, Christie, sent him this copy of a painting in the George District of South Africa. He felt that the headdresses of the figures were so unusual that they must depict foreigners, but, in fact, this way of rendering the head is merely one of the many conventions used by the painters to disguise human features. (Photo by Stella Mayes Reed.)

dispel the mystery. Dolman, a young German explorer who followed up some of the routes discovered by Livingstone, copied some of the paintings that he discovered in Botswana. Neither Livingstone nor his father-in-law, Moffat, seem to have been interested in rock painting, but they did leave us many invaluable first-hand accounts of the Bushmen themselves before these actors staged their last performance on the African scene.

Hitherto, most rock paintings had been discovered in areas where the Bushmen were either still painting or that they had left only recently. A whole crop of discoveries now began to be made all over Africa, some of them in areas so far from the present-day haunts of the Bushmen that it seemed impossible that there could be any connection between them and the little people, some of them in regions, so arid and desolate that it was difficult to imagine the time when they could have had any inhabitants whatsoever.

In 1847, a party of French officers who were exploring in Southern Oran, in North Africa, reported their discovery of rock engravings depicting animals that had long disappeared from the region — lions, elephants, ostriches, antelopes, cattle, and gazelles — together with pictures of archers.

The German explorer Heinrch Barth, who was crossing the Sahara from Tripoli in North Africa to Timbuktu on the Niger, found more engravings of a similar sort in the Fezzan. The import of these discoveries could hardly be lost on those who evaluated them. The engravings, with the paintings that were later to be found alongside them, were in such arid spots that the abundant fauna depicted in them must surely date to a very remote period indeed.

Though the examination of rock paintings in Africa hitherto had been carried out in a very perfunctory way, it had established several very important facts. As has already been noticed, work was still going on at some of the painted surfaces or it has stopped quite recently. This could be seen from pictures that depicted subjects that could only be contemporary, such as paintings of men on horseback. More important still, perhaps, though many of the paintings described by early travelers have been lost, others have survived to our own day and are quite discernible, suggesting that the painting media used were so good that the pictures have remained, unchanged, down to our own day. Thus, one painting noticed by Sir J. E. Alexander in 1836 was described by Alexander R. Willcox in 1959.

The era of early discovery had closed and that of systematic recording was now about to begin. The idea of recording paintings was due solely to the work of an untaught, or rather self-taught, English working man, George William Stow, whose record of achievement reads like a story out of Samuel Smiles's *Self Help*, that bible for Victorian self-made men. The fact that Stow never made a penny out of his life's work of recording African paintings need not bother us, as it probably never troubled him. A Warwickshire lad, Stow had come to South Africa as a trader and geological surveyor. His interest in rocks promoted an interest in the rock engravings and paintings and he began to travel through the Eastern Province of Cape Colony, Griqualand West, and the Orange Free State, copying all those he could find that interested him. Like many self-taught men, Stow was a man of strong views, well able to strike out for himself and plan the direction that his life should take. What that plan was can best be seen from a letter that he wrote to a friend in 1870.

"During the last three years," he said, "I have been making pilgrimages to the various old Bushman caves among the mountains in this part of the colony [Queenstown] and Kaffraria, and as their paintings are becoming obliterated very fast, it struck me that it would be well to make copies of them before these interesting relics of an almost extinct race are entirely destroyed. This gave rise to the idea in my mind of collecting material enough to complete a history of the manners and customs of the Bushmen as depicted by themselves. I have fortunately been able to procure many facsimile copies of hunting scenes, dances, fightings, etc., showing the modes of warfare, the chase, weapons, disguises, etc."[6]

From one point of view, Stow's methodical outlook on the paintings, and the question that he kept asking himself, "What has this painting got to teach me, for my history?," was disastrous. He became convinced that every painting had its message, and that it was necessary to unravel that message. This prompted him to put leading questions to his Bushmen informers, questions that they were quick to answer, for Africans are nothing if not polite, and as contemporary travelers complained, if they did not know the answer to a question they would make one up, so as not to disappoint their interlocutor. Stow also suffered from another working defect. He never copied all the paintings in a cave, only a figure here and there. He would select particular figures, retaining proportional spaces between those which formed a group. Hence, it is possible, at least, to speculate that the figures that he left out of his copy might give us grounds to refute the interpretation that he put on the picture, or that he derived from his Bushmen informants. Such criticisms sound ungrateful, when applied to the father of African rupestral art, but they are directed at defects that were in no way detrimental to the greatness of his total work.

Stow's method of copying pictures was to make a preliminary copy on rough paper, then trace from the rough copy a design onto a sheet of art paper. Sometimes, he was so short of suitable paper on which to draw that he would reproduce figures from different parts of a cave, or even from different shelters, onto one and the same sheet. Once he had drawn the design on the art paper he next colored it, and he used as his paints the original Bushman pigments, which he picked up from the floor of the cave where he had been copying. In spite of the difficulties with which he contended, such as the painfully slow progress by ox wagon from site to site, Stow had an advantage that no other copyist has enjoyed. He had a little Bushboy as his helper, who enabled him to find caves. His helper also prepared the backgrounds for his pictures, and suggested interpretations of the subjects. The Bushmen, and Africans generally, have a much better eye for country than any European. When they want to, they can suggest caves of which no white man would ever be aware. We can be sure that Stow was able to make good use of his helper. At the end of his life, in 1882, the seventy-four-year-old Warwickshire man left behind him a precious heritage of seventy-four cartoons. They were to be his permanent contribution to Bushman art, and the nucleus round which all the other copies that have been made since were to grow, though Stow himself possibly regarded his book on the native races of South Africa as more important than his copies.

Though there are plenty of rock paintings that he never copied, and never knew about, his work remains definitive in that many of his shelters have now been stripped of their paintings. They have been cut out and removed for collectors or museums, destroyed by rock falls, badly blurred by "foliation," the flaking off of the rock surface, the rubbing of animals penned in the caves, or the deposition of soot from fires. Rain has washed them out or otherwise so dimmed them that they are very far from being the paintings Stow copied. Nonetheless, no one, apparently, has undertaken such a seemingly obvious task as photographing the originals with an infrared film so as to check whether they are true copies, and also to discover what has been left out.

Stow's exposition of the paintings that he copied was regarded with considerable respect during his lifetime and for a long time afterwards because wherever possible he tried to interpret them by asking his Bushman acquaintances what they meant. These Bushman interpretations of the paintings were received almost as gospel at the time, but I shall try to

[6]Dorothea F. Bleek, *Rock Paintings in South Africa* (London: Methuen, 1930), p. 26.

suggest that it would be extremely unwise to accept them at their face value.

Meanwhile, it is worth noting that Stow's magnificent example of a life spent in pursuit of rock paintings did not find the echo that might have been expected from South Africa. It took longer for the paintings to get published than it had taken for Stow to make the cartoons. The resulting long delay between production and publication undoubtedly held up the progress of rock art studies. When publication did come, in 1930, it was due to the generosity of another expatriate, the American Andrew Carnegie, as well as to the tenacious energy of Stow's literary executors. Bushman studies may indeed be said to be much more indebted to America rather than to South Africa, because it was Americans who financed the publication of the Dictionary of the Bushman language, the foundation for the linguistic studies that are still being made in the language of the living Bushmen of the Kalahari (apparently representatives of tribes other than those which were exterminated in the Drakensberg) as well as into the many volumes of Bushman folklore recorded by Wilhelm Immanuel Bleek.

Bleek had been a close friend of Stow's and the two men had in common that they were both prepared to shoulder what would have seemed impossible tasks to anyone else. Bleek, a German scholar in an era when it was considered that the only real scholars were Germans, had come out to the Cape to work as an archivist. Before long he had decided that he would devote his life to the study of the fast-disappearing Bushman language, and the recording of Bushman folklore. Almost all the mythological interpretations that have been placed on Bushman paintings rest on the material contained in the notebooks in which Bleek set down his conversations with the Bushmen, especially those Bushmen who had been let out of prison on parole and been allowed to work for him as his household servants. Many of Bleek's friends must have considered that he was a bold man in thus taking his house boys from the Breakwater Prison, but the Bushboys proved ideal servants and were devoted to the family. In fact, they were too devoted. They cleaned the table knives so vigorously that half the blades and a whole bath brick disappeared in a month. Dorothea Bleek, the daughter of the folklorist, records that the Bushmen were very fond of animals—one of them wept when his puppy had distemper. They were also passionately fond of music, telling stories and acting them out. At first Bleek had hired an ex-warder with a gun to keep watch over the prisoners, a precaution that soon proved unnecessary. He was able to begin recording their language and folklore as he now spoke Bushman and some of the servants spoke Afrikaans or English. Dorothea records with astonishment that some of the Bushmen could not understand each other's speech, a fact that suggests that they may have had very divergent traditions with regard to paintings as well. Bleek worked so hard at his self-imposed task that it is hardly a surprise to learn that he died at the early age of forty-eight. His sister-in-law, Miss Lucy Lloyd, not only carried on his life's work but encouraged Stow in his. At his death she bought his drawings, thus probably saving them for posterity. After her death, in 1914, she willed them to Dorothea, Bleek's youngest daughter, and Dorothea, in her turn, gave a noble example of persistence in the family tradition by publishing *Rock Paintings in South Africa from Parts of the Eastern Province and Orange Free State,*[7] just fifty years after Stow's death. It was a work composed entirely from his paintings.

Though there was an undoubted lack of funds for research into rock painting, shortage of cash was, to some extent, compensated for by the burning enthusiasm with which many South Africans took up the task of recording their national heritage.

Scholars, such as Maria Wilman, who published *Rock Engravings of Griqualand West and Bechuanaland,* in 1933, turned into explorers, bumping over rocky tracks in ox carts so as to try to discover new painted sites. Civil engineers, such as Professor C. van Riet Lowe, fell under the sway of the painter's art and devoted their lives to archaeological research. Even troopers in the police, such as J. A. Hill and A. D. Whyte, spent months among the hills recording new rock sites.

Hitherto, students of the rock paintings had been dependent on colored or black and white copies that had been published in some of the rare books to appear on the subject — such as Helen Tongue's *Bushman Paintings,* which had come out in 1909.[8] Painted records of the paintings had to be supplemented by photographs, however. Both media were complementary to one another. Good drawings offered a sympathetic attempt to reconstruct the original picture, but, every copy is a subjective

[7]Ibid.

[8]M. Helen Tongue, *Bushman Paintings* (Oxford: Clarendon Press, 1909).

Men with caps, karosses (skin coats), and sticks, with
a bird-headed man. (Painting by Helen Tongue. Photo
by Stella Mayes Reed.)

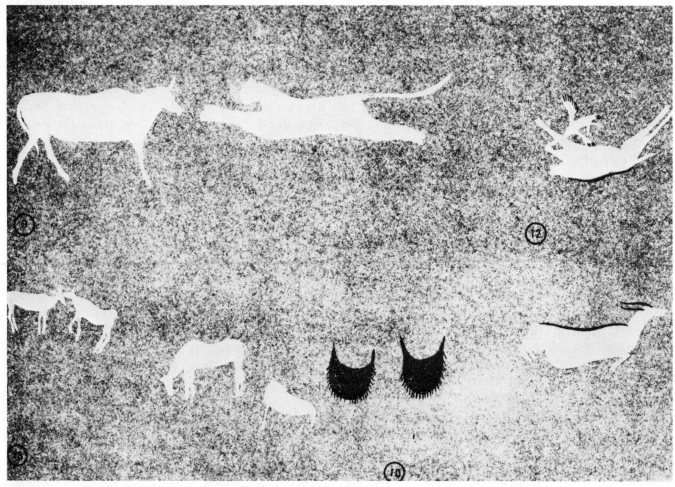

A leopard springing on an ox, eland, and two fringed
aprons, from Bufelstein. (Painting by Helen Tongue.
Photo by Stella Mayes Reed.)

Wild beast chasing a man, a woman, and a boy. (Painting by Helen Tongue. Photo by Stella Mayes Reed.)

Men with bows and arrows, and women danci (Painting by Helen Tongue. Photo by Stella Ma Reed.)

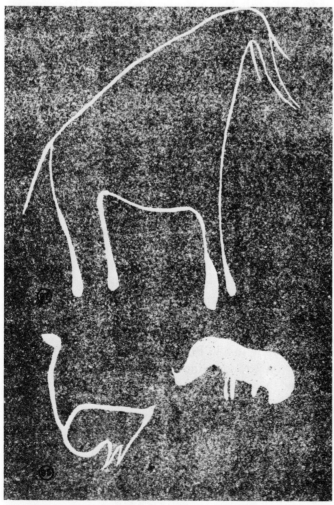

Ostrich, rhinoceros, and elephant. (Painting by Helen Tongue. Photo by Stella Mayes Reed.)

Bucks, doe, hare, and jackal. (Painting by Helen Tongue. Photo by Stella Mayes Reed.)

Animals and monsters attacking hunters. (Painting by Helen Tongue. Photo by Stella Mayes Reed.)

interpretation, which imposes on what are often very faded and imperfectly preserved painting lines, features, volume, and shading, which may not have been present in the original artist's intention, but may have been suggested by some feature of the cave, such as a crack in the rock surface.

Good photographs will display what is actually on the rock to the beholder's eye and leave him to make his own reconstruction. They can also see below the rock surface by using infrared light. Furthermore, the mere physical demands of recording rock paintings demands photography, since one cannot always travel accompanied by a staff of artists, as did Frobenius.

The first photograph of a rock painting was taken by von Bonde in 1885, and just over ten years later, photography of rock paintings had become so common that instructions were being sent out to amateur photographers on how to set about recording them on film. Therefore, the real interpreter and exponent of African rock paintings has become the photographer. It is he, much more than the scholar, who stands between the painters of antiquity and the art lovers of today. The privilege of walking the rock galleries of Africa is not given to everyone — most of us have to be content with good photographs. Moreover, the continent is so vast that it would be impossible for any observer to see all the paintings there.

It is now necessary to turn aside for a moment from the current of investigations into rock art in Africa to see what effect the discoveries had produced on Europe. Between Stow's arrival in South Africa in 1842 and his death forty years later, the rock paintings had attracted enough attention to have been made the subject of articles in magazines, and to have been exhibited in London. There was nothing unusual in all this. If there was one country in which the British public took an interest, it was South Africa. It was here that British expansion had received one of its most severe checks in the shape of a defeat at the hands of the Boers at Majuba Hill in 1881 near the Drakensberg, where painting had just stopped. The Boers would probably not have fought if the menace of the Zulus had not been removed by breaking them as a military power, though not before they had inflicted a severe defeat at Isandlwana. During the fighting Napoleon III's son, the Prince Imperial, had been killed, and some time previously a very intelligent Zulu witch doctor had pointed out to Bishop Colenso that the Bible must have an allegorical, not a literal, meaning, because the stores laid in by Noah were woefully inadequate to feed the animals aboard. Small wonder that Disraeli exclaimed, "Remarkable people, these Zulus. They defeat our regiments, they convert our bishops, and now they have put an end to a dynasty," or that British interest in all things South African should be strong.

Thomas Baines, whom we have already met, capitalized on this interest by putting some of his paintings of the country on show at the Colonial and Indian Exhibition in London in 1886. Also on show was a real Bushman painting that had been transported to London. It was a painted seal's bone, decorated with designs of birds and seals in black, which is now in the British Museum. Other Bushman art was on show in the shape of a painted boulder that had been collected by E. J. Dunn and that was

Eland from Baviaans Krantz. (Painting by Helen Tongue. Photo by Stella Mayes Reed.)

Game and a hunter. (Painting by Helen Tongue.   Photo by Stella Mayes Reed.)

possibly the first Bushman painting to travel abroad. It was certainly not the last, because, for the Victorians, to admire was to covet. Special shops existed to cater to the collectors of ethnographical treasures and the demand now grew for pieces of Bushman art. Museums, as well as collectors, were eager to secure specimens. In 1893, Louis E. Tylor removed some paintings from the rock shelters of the Drakensberg and sent them, along with copies of other paintings, to the Pitt-Rivers Museum at Oxford. Emil Holub, at the end of one of his books about Africa, had regretted that he had been unable to bring home any "Bushman engravings." He more than made up for this omission on a subsequent expedition, in 1881, removing some paintings and many engravings to Vienna. An illustration shows his men at work. The rocky hillside is littered with the guns and knapsacks of the party. Under the watchful gaze of Holub a fire crackles brightly at the base of a rock bearing an engraving. The stone must be red hot, for

an African helper is dashing buckets of water over it, so that the contraction will split the rock face away from the parent block. A man in checked trousers, shirt, and bowler hat is hammering a chisel into a crack that is developing behind the face of a rock that holds an engraving. A companion watches him, nursing a bottle in his hand, for it is obviously thirsty work. A third man hammers wedges into a crack in another engraved rock, using a sledge hammer to drive the wedges home. Two more tug and pull with crowbars at a half-removed engraving. All that is wanting in this illustration of Holub at work is some indication of his failures—the five or six engraved rocks that he must have ruined in order to get one whole engraving back to Vienna.

Collectors such as Tylor and Holub found only too many imitators, and many rock paintings and engravings, collected by unscrupulous dealers and sold to European museums or collectors, have now simply disappeared. Even sadder than the theft of such

38

treasures was the growth of vandalism — which appears to be a vice confined to "progressive" civilizations. Although Basuto herdsmen scraped off the paint on the cave walls where it was thick to use as a medicine (just as in England country folk scraped the alabaster figures in tombs and gave the parings to their cows if they were ill) the Bantu had left the paintings severely alone. The increasing white population of South Africa put an end to this immunity "The fine cave near Ceres," wrote Dr. George Theal in 1878, "is now covered with travellers' and visitors' names in black paint."[9]

In spite of discouragements such as the growing destruction of rock paintings and the realization that there would be no more, since those Bushmen who had escaped the massacres and taken refuge in the Kalahari had now definitely stopped painting, art lovers and archaeologists in the republic pressed on with their work. The technique of making painted copies of rock pictures improved, as it became obvious that no photograph could be all sufficient. The camera could not look around corners and many rock paintings were spread over a very irregularly shaped shelter roof so that they could not be photographed in one exposure. It was now being realized that a good painted copy could help by, for example, filtering out unwanted aspects of the present-day appearance of the paintings such as a growth of efflorescence from the cave wall. It is possible at this point to look ahead to the copying that is still being done in South Africa under government auspices. The paintings are traced, life size, from the cave walls, onto a transparent sheet. Another tracing is then made from this master sheet onto art paper. The background and figures are then colored so as to be an exact match for the original, and the finished cartoon is then filed in a cabinet.

Painted copies of rock pictures were to find superb expression, in 1959, in one of the most impressive books ever dedicated to rock painting.[10] Before further reference is made to it, however, it is necessary to look at the progress of rock studies in Rhodesia.

As early as 1899, A.J.C. Molyneux had contributed a paper on rock paintings to the *Proceedings of the Rhodesia Scientific Association.* By 1912, R.N. Hall

had worked out the superposition of many of the paintings by older ones. 1929 saw an event of considerable importance for the study of rock art in Africa as a whole. In the excavation of the Bambata Cave, during that year, it now appeared possible to demonstrate a connection between a particular stage of archaeological development, the Wilton Culture, and an era in cave painting. During the same year, an expedition under Dr. Frobenius visited both Rhodesia and South Africa. In contrast to Stow, Frobenius had no difficulty in getting really generous help from the South African government. South Africa gave him £16,000 to enable him to employ a team of seven artists to copy the rock paintings. Rhodesia gave him free railroad transport. Yet, the results of such a

Emil Holub, the Austrian Africanist, was one of the first to draw attention to the rock engravings. In this illustration, he shows Bushmen executing the petraglyphs with sharply pointed stones.

[9] J. and I. Rudner, *The Hunter and His Art,* p. 261.

[10] Elizabeth Goodall, C. K. Cooke, and J. Desmond Clark, *Prehistoric Rock Art of the Federation of Rhodesia and Nyasaland* (Glasgow: University Press, 1959).

promising expedition were overclouded. Frobenius summed up his conclusions in two books, *Madzimu Dsangara*[11] and *Erythraa.*[12] Neither of his two works seem to have found English translators, and since the purpose of the books was ethnographic rather than artistic, their effect in bringing rock art before a wider public was rather secondary. Only a number of the paintings that were copies of the rock frescoes were presented to the sponsor nations who had financed the expedition, and much of the material amassed was destroyed in Berlin during World War II. Questions were asked in the South African Parliament about why such generosity had been shown to Frobenius, and the reply was that Frobenius's work had been spread over a number of years and that help had been forthcoming from the German government as well. The Frobenius expedition may well be held to mark the coming of age of African rupestral studies in that they had hitherto been considered in a local context, or had attracted attention in the parent country of the colony, England. Here they were now being examined by a scholar of European repute. The age of international expeditions in search of rock art had now begun. It continued with the visit of the Abbé Breuil in 1947. The Abbé had done so much work on rock paintings in Europe, the Sahara, and Ethiopia that it was not to be expected that he would neglect the southern parts of the continent. In 1947, accompanied by the veteran South African archaeologist Professor van Riet Lowe, the Abbé made a tour of the rock sites. Whatever his faults as an archaeologist, Breuil certainly did not lack the determination to carry out his research in the face of advancing age or the persistence to publish them. The motto of so many archaeologists, "Dig now, publish never," was not for him. Nor did he lack the courage to put forward hypotheses that were startling in their originality and that perhaps earned for him the hostility of those who never liked to commit themselves to any viewpoint at all. If he did nothing else, the Abbé certainly stung homegrown Africanists into renewed activity. In 1959, decades of patient labor by Rhodesian scholars bore fruit in a monumental volume in the best tradition of academic scholarship, combined with the fine artistic renderings in which working man George William Stow had shown the way. It was a threefold account of the three countries that then made up the Federation of Rhodesia —

[11] Leo Frobenius, *Madzimu Dsangara*, Berlin, 1932.
[12] Leo Frobenius, *Erythraa*, Berlin, 1932.

Southern Rhodesia (Rhodesia), Northern Rhodesia (now Zambia), and Nyasaland (now Malawi). Some agreement was reached by the three authors even if they could not agree on all points, such as the interpretations of the schematic paintings. Whatever views one may take on the conclusions of the consortium, their illustrations, especially those of the abstract paintings, will always remain a delight to those who are even faintly interested in African art.

In East Africa, Dr. and Mrs. Leakey followed up the efforts of earlier explorers, such as F. B. Bagshawe, T.A.M. Nash, A. T. Culwick, and R.D.H. Arundell, in trying to locate all and, if possible, excavate some of the painted shelters that abound in that region. Meanwhile, other workers in the Horn of Africa and in Ethiopia continued to increase the already impressive corpus of known rock shelters. At Lago Oda and north of Harar, important discoveries were made by Père P. Azais and Count Björn von Rosen.

The main interest among the public in rock art had now swung northwards, however, as the riches of the Sahara began to be apparent. Though frescoes and engravings had been discovered in the Hoggar, Algieria, as early as the 1900s and, although the indefatigable Frobenius and Reygasse had worked in North Africa during the thirties it was left for the expeditions that centered around the middle of the century to unfold the existence of the true wealth of Saharan art.

Lieutenant Brenans explored at least twelve Saharan localities, and although the written notes of his expeditions, with their interpretations of the paintings, have drawn the considerable criticism of his fellow countrymen, who are not always so restrained as Anglo-Saxon archaeologists, his merit as a discoverer remains entire. The real Columbus of Saharan art, however, is Henri Lhote, who made expeditions to about fourteen different sites. M. M. Verriale searched upwards of nine, while Mlle. Yolande Tschudi, a Swiss ethnographer who had been diverted from her study of the Touareg through their migration southward, due to drought, was diverted to the study of the paintings of Tassili, of which she made a definitive survey between 1950 and 1951.

Meanwhile, the argument over the dating of rock art, which had been carried out largely on comparative or stylistic grounds, was now moving into the scientific plane with the discovery of multiple methods whereby the age of a rock painting might be arrived at. During the 1970s, Dr. E. Denninger has tried to determine the age of the paintings by discovering whether the fixatives mixed with the pigments in the paints contained albumen, as some of them did, and then determining the decrease in the amino acids that the albumen contained. Unfortunately, this dating method only provides dates of up to 1800 years ago.

Even more striking results were obtained by dating the carbon pigments, or the archaeological remains that contained carbon, which are associated with particular painted caves. There is still room for some doubt even in scientific methods such as these. A piece of carbon with which a painter drew his picture on the wall may have been fossil charcoal, which he unearthed from a deposit in the floor of the cave. We know from accounts of surviving Bushmen that painters did dig up their colors. The dates given for the dessication of the Sahara, after which the paintings must have ceased, are also approximate rather than exact, but it is something to have even an approximation to hard facts in the shifting sands that constitute so much of rock art studies.

2

The Problem of the Paintings

Part of the fascination of the study of rock art comes from the fact that just to look at a single painting raises all sorts of mysteries. The example has already been given of the *White Lady of the Brandberg,* and the problem of infibulation raised. Did human beings ever really voluntarily submit to one of the cruellest self-inflicted mutilations ever devised? Everything is possible when it comes to the vagaries of male fashion. The Hottentots, after all, are accused by contemporary travelers of partially castrating themselves, and one heretical sect, the *Skoptsi,* did carry out complete self-castration in Russia during the nineteenth century. Yet the alternative to believing in infibulation is to believe that the rock painters pictured taboo symbols in their paintings.

Yet infibulation is only a specific problem and hardly of any importance compared with the more general ones. There are quite a number of these, and perhaps the most important is the sheer wealth of known examples of the painters' art. The number of paintings and engravings that invite examination and comparison are vast, even in an area such as central Africa, which is by no means as rich as the Sahara.

In 1959, it was estimated that there were more than 1,100 painted sites in Rhodesia, Malawi, and Zambia, about 1,600 on South Africa, with twenty-nine rock engraving sites in the three countries mentioned above and another 350 in South Africa. Recent discoveries have, of course, added very much to the problem by increasing the number of known sites, but even as it existed sixteen years ago the problem was considerable in that it was impossible to visit every site personally, while on the other hand there was no central bank of rock art data. Often, textbooks on rock art have been filled in, in part, merely on the observation notes compiled by various travelers who had visited a site. Though musuem collections are often very rich in photographs of rock art—principally, I feel, because there is, nowadays very little art of any other kind to be recorded in Africa—it is extremely doubtful whether any museum, or group of museums, could have put together enough photographs to illustrate all the known paintings in the Federations of the Rhodesias, as it then was, a number that may be estimated as being in the nature of about eleven thousand examples. Hence, the difficulty in coming to a really definitive conclusion about the art of the three countries. Although something is being done to remedy this state of affairs in South Africa, where a complete copy of all known examples is being made, this will, even when completed, be of merely national value. What is wanted is a center of rock art studies for the whole of Africa. Yet given prevailing conditions in Africa, it is very unlikely that such a center will ever be set up.

By comparison with the Sahara, Malawi, Rhodesia, Zambia, and South Africa are easy countries in which to travel. They have been much more thoroughly explored than the Saharan sites probably ever will be, and they have also been made the subject of considerable excavation. Excavation in the Sahara, though not impossible, is rendered difficult because of the absence of water.

Not merely is there a distinct possibility that discoveries in new sites may overturn everything that we now believe about rock painting, but there were so many painters at work at one time that it must have been very difficult for all of them to paint according to the rules of the school. What these were will hopefully be discovered later. There must have always been painters, here and there, who were so provincial, so out of touch, that their work could be considered as aberrant. Yet, a fresco by even one of these painters might destroy the belief in all the generalities that have been building up through comparison to work of all the other painters, or it might even be impossible to apply *any* rules to rock paintings at all.

An example of the exception that oversets all the supposed rules is the portrayal of totemistic animals. Elsewhere, I argue that the paintings could not have been totemistic in origin because one of the principal animals to play a part in Bushman folklore never appears. This is the Hyrax, also called the Dassie or Rock Rabbit. Like all general statements that refer to rock art, this one uses "never" in the Gilbertian sense of "hardly ever." In part of a frieze illustrated by Elizabeth Goodall[1] what may be a rock rabbit appears, clutched by a giant figure.

If there are too many sites to be examined that are constantly being added to on the one hand, other old ones, to which one would like to refer or recur, are constantly disappearing. The African continent is still clay in the hands of the potter, and the rock sites are exposed to a continuous attrition by the hands of nature. In the Sahara, wind-blown sand acts as a sandblast that grinds the pictures and engravings slowly away from the face of the rock. Further south, in central and southern Africa, the pictures have been painted on igneous rocks, which are crystalline in

structure, and which are, therefore, particularly liable to fracture—if, that is, they were not badly fractured already during their cooling and crystallization in origin. Throughout the day, the crust of the rock is warmed by the sun. Then, as sunset falls, in a matter of minutes, the rock face is abruptly exposed to a cooling process. The alternate heat and cold of day and night set up expansion and contraction and in the face of this to and fro movement the rock begins to "exfoliate." Pieces of the surface become fractured in a curve, which eventually breaks off the rock and falls away, bringing with it any paintings on the surface. This process, which is gradually whittling away the number of painted sites available for study, does at least provide the possibility of dating. It has been calculated that exfoliation proceeds at such a pace that the very earliest Stone Age folk of Central and Southern Africa cannot have contributed to our corpus of rock paintings, since none of their work could have survived, due to the rate of exfoliation.

Not merely does the rock canvas of the paintings split and crack continually, it is changing in other ways as well. The rock is becoming weathered, undergoing a process of oxydization in which the newly exposed surface of dolerite or sandstone gradually acquires a new skin of iron oxide. Weathering can fill in the lines of an engraving, making it well-nigh invisible. It can also dim the colors of a painting, obliterating them or giving them an appearance of false antiquity.

Men have lent a hand in the process of giving the rocks a patina. Hordes of successive sightseers have splashed the rock with water to bring up the color of the paintings or rubbed it with halves of lemons. Sometimes, the painting has merely faded, moving further back into the rock, but, in other instances, the whole surface has become clouded over with a thin, transparent film that comes in between the observer and the art. This is just what has happened to the painting of the *White Lady of the Brandberg.*

The one process that one would feel ought to have set in the frescoes, general fading, does not seem to have taken place at all. True, one cannot be sure what has faded and what has not until the rock sites are photographed systematically with infrared film. Nonetheless, it has been pointed out more than once already that some paintings appear to be as fresh now as they were when they were first discovered. Why should this be the case? One reason lies in the very skilled technique used to mix the paints, and this will be discussed later. Another reason lies with the choice

[1] Goodall, Cooke, and Clark, *Prehistoric Rock Art of the Federation of Rhodesia and Nyasaland,* p. 17.

The artist thought the main figure in this picture that she copied at Greenvale was smoking. To me, it appears self-evident that she is playing a musical bow, and the dots are the notes of the song that she is playing. Which of us is right? (Painting by Helen Tongue. Photo by Stella Mayes Reed.)

of the site of the painting, (sunny, but not too exposed) and the fastness of the colors used. Red ochre, which carpets the ground for hundreds of yards in part of the Sahara, has lain bleaching under the sun for so many million years that it is hardly likely to lose any color once applied to a rock wall in the form of paint.

One natural problem remains to be mentioned. Since the rock on which the paintings were made is rarely unified and smooth, the projecting angularities have become incorporated, as it were, in our view of the painting. Did the painter cleverly make use of these knobs and jagged points of the cave roof, or were they an aspect of the picture that, by convention we are meant to ignore, just as nowadays we ignore the frame of a picture?

Archaeology has done so much to establish at least tentative dates for all the great schools of rock painting that it seems almost ungrateful to complain that the archaeologists have answered none of the questions to which we would really like the answer.

In this Rhodesian painting, a hunter grasps his bow. The "infibulated penis" may either be a portrayal of a real item of dress, or a sexual taboo symbol. (Photo Courtesy Rhodesian Ministry of Information.)

The problems of copying the paintings in a vast cave such as this Zambian one at Nashu are considerable, while interpretation is rendered more difficult by the fact that it is impossible to mount a "mock up" or the completed tracings or drawings in exactly the way in which they appeared in the cave. (Courtesy Zambian Tourist Board.)

The archaeological background in Africa is so different from that in Europe that it is not surprising that the task of connecting paintings with archaeological investigation has set more problems than it has solved. While in Europe, the stone age ended some thousands of years ago, it still continues in Africa in areas like the Kalahari. Until quite recently, there was nothing to stop a contemporary African from picking up a handaxe and using it, first having sharpened it on the grooved wall of a cave in the way in which one of the very early hunter artists would have done. It is perfectly possible to imagine Bantu herdsmen, trapped in a rock shelter by torrential rain, rummaging about on the floor of the shelter until they found a piece of charcoal — perhaps even a piece of fossil charcoal — and then beginning to draw a picture

on the wall with it. How was this picture to be fitted in, by archaeologists, with the drawings made perhaps thousands of years ago with other similar charcoal or ochre crayons? The imitative element is strong in everyone as can be seen from the desire of modern tourists to write their names, or even make little drawings, next to the cave paintings. Many of the paintings that are so hard to classify were probably made by imitators, perhaps children, in this way, but there is no way of knowing just when.

Dating and classifying the cave paintings of Europe was an easy task by comparison with the same process in Africa. The two situations were completely different. Some elements of cave art in Europe, such as sculpture, were entirely absent. Extinct animals depicted in the cave paintings of Europe were a great help toward dating them, because it was known, approximately, when the last mammoth had died, so if a mammoth appeared in a cave painting, it could instantly be assigned a rough date. There are some extinct fauna in the African cave paintings, such as the Mediterranean deer, which traveled south as far as

Kasamba Stream Grinding Grooves. (Photo Courtesy Zambian National Tourist Bureau.)

Ethiopia. Unfortunately, deer, like the quagga, seem to have been alive while most of the paintings were made and to have become extinct only in very recent times. One deer is even depicted in a medieval painting in an Ethiopian church. It has, however, been possible to suggest likely dates for the southward movement of game from the Sahara in view of its progressive drying out, and the beginning of the dry period has been dated approximately.

Perhaps the biggest drawback archaeologists have had to face in Africa has been the absence of what French archaeologists called *art mobilier*, small portable carvings and engravings. Sometimes, the themes on these pieces of carved bone or ivory were reproduced on the painted surfaces of the caves, and it was, therefore, an easy matter to refer a particular style of painting to a specific archaelogical level.

There is no use looking for inscriptions in Central or Southern Africa as an aid to elucidating the mystery of cave painting, but paradoxically, inscriptions do occur in the caves of the Sahara. Quite long legends in Libyco Berber script are to be found there, as well as in the rock shelters of the Grand Kabylie. What do they mean? We do not know, because although the Libyco Berber script has been taken

These engravings are almost certainly "functional". They were cut so as to facilitate the shaping of the edge of stone axes. (Photo Courtesy of Zambian Tourist Agency.)

Elands, and Quagga. The quagga is the only important extinct animal among the repertoire of southern and central African painters. (Painting by Helen Tongue. Photo by Stella Mayes Reed.)

over by the modern Touareg, its old meaning remains unknown. It is at least possible to speculate that the legends are the abbreviated form of what the paintings had to say. Just as in cave painting in another part of the world, Buddha would be represented first as a symbol, because he is too holy to be portrayed, and would, in time, be made the subject of a painting, until finally the religious message depicted both by symbol and picture would have added to it a written prayer in Chinese. So it is not inconceivable that the characters written in the caves of North Africa and the Sahara have some strong connection with the paintings that preceded them. Until the discovery of a "Rosetta Stone" that transliterates the lost script, this hypothesis will have to remain purely speculative.

If there is no Rosetta Stone in African rock art, there is no Solutré or Aurignac-classic French prehistoric cave sites either. Many painted caves have been dug by archaeologists without publication of the results and sometimes with the total loss of the objects recovered. Others have been disturbed by

A wounded bear climbs a palm tree in this painting from a farm in the Goromonzi Area of Rhodesia, where now neither bears nor palm trees are to be found. This is a very unusual subject in cave art. (Photo Courtesy Rhodesian Ministry of Information.)

47

guano hunters, while a disappointingly high proportion have stone floors in which it is hopeless to look for any archaeological deposits at all. Those of the Brandberg, in some ways the most interesting of all rock art areas, because it was the last to undergo painting, are a case in point.

It is very rare to find a cave such as Bambata in Rhodesia, where objects have been found that can be dated in comparison with the paintings. A cave such as Kisese in Tanzania, where there is a combination of deep archaeological remains and other factors that help in dating, is rarer still. At Kisese, a piece of the cave wall broke away and fell to the floor, covering an occupation layer associated with the lower Stone Age. The part of the wall where the break had taken place had been painted. The deposits covered by the

broken-off slab had been laid down by cavedwellers who practiced iron working, which indicated a comparatively late date for the cave paintings, one measured in centuries rather than millenia. On top, the deposit layer had built up to a total depth of twenty feet. Such easily dated cave paintings are extremely rare.

Archaeological finds have been helpful, in part. They have helped to relate the paintings to the life of the past. One very frequent discovery in a cave investigation, for example, is the painter's equipment. This can take the form of broken iron nodules with the rust red powder still inside, or stone mortars and pestles that were used for grinding up the red ochre and other mineral colors.

Ostrich-shell beads are another very frequent dis-

Rock painting from "Diana's Vow" Cave, near Rusape on the main Umtali in Rhodesia. The subject of the picture may be a ceremonial burial. Note the figures decorated with white ostrich shell beads or paint. (Photo Courtesy Rhodesian Department of Information.)

48

covery at cave sites. Beads of this sort appear to be worn by many of the figures. The flint burins, gravers, and adzes that chipped and scratched out the engravings are to be found at many levels, along with other stone artifacts such as arrowheads, similar to those which appear in the paintings, and the stone weights for digging sticks, which women in the paintings are portrayed using or carrying. Painted stones have been discovered in South African caves, but no painted walls, suggesting that, after all, there may have been more than one school of art throughout this vast region. Flaked-off painted roofs and walls have also been discovered, covered by later occupation layers, suggesting that, as has been inferred elsewhere, exfoliation has robbed us of the earliest treasures of cave paintings. One of the most interesting discoveries of the archaeologist has been that some painted caves were occupied, indeed continuously occupied, from Stone Age down to Iron Age times. Does the existence of cooking pots and discarded household refuse destroy the hypothesis I shall try to form later, that the caves were essentially shrines? Cooking utensils have been interpreted as evidence of domesticity, but there is no reason why they should not have been used for sacrifice. Moreri talks about the Hottentots offering libations of milk to their god, who lives "on high." Furthermore, the existence of a shrine presupposes that of a priesthood, who were presumably resident.

Though archaeological research has suggested that two principal types of early Africans were coincidental with the cave paintings, Wilton and Nachikufuan Man, skeletal remains of the men associated with these two stages of development, are very scanty, so in an attempt to learn more about the artist hunters, scholars have examined with some care the profiles and figures of the people whose protraits appear in the cave paintings.

Just because the ancient Egyptians — who obviously owe a cultural debt to the hunter painters — were such skilled portrayers of racial types that one can instantly pick out the different subject races of the Egyptian Empire (four of whom appear supporting Tutankhamen's footstool), one might hope to get the same insight into racial types in the rock frescoes.

Here the picture is very muddled, however, for two principal reasons. The rock artists felt inhibited when they came to represent a human face. Possibly, like the ancient Egyptians, they believed that if you drew someone's portrait, you created a sort of spiritual twin of the sitter. Anything that happened to the portrait would in some way affect the sitter — an idea that has a long life and is still to some extent observable in European folklore, as well as finding literary expression in *The Portrait of Dorian Gray*, by Oscar Wilde. To the Egyptians, a happy portrait would be that which continued to regard placidly all the good things painted round about him — cattle, servants preparing beer, wives and concubines, houses and gardens. An unhappy portrait on the other hand would be one that could no longer behold these good things. If one had an enemy, he made a point of slipping into his tomb and scratching out the eyes of his portrait on the wall, or even destroying the regarding figure of himself that was usually contained in the tomb as well. The Bushman was certainly much concerned lest he should reveal enough of his personal identity to enable anyone to work magic against him. It was for this reason, presumably, that he would never tell anyone his name — those Bushmen whose real names we do know belong to the very last period of Bushman development outside the Kalahari. Though the cave painters of the Sahara had not observed the rule that all figures should be faceless wholeheartedly, they were undoubtedly influenced by it. Their early figures are "aniconic" or faceless, while in the later ones the faces are often drawn in a rather blurred or impersonal way, so that they could be the faces of anyone. Sexual traits are often omitted. This was one way of rendering a portrait "anonymous." The picture of a man could hardly be a real portrait if his virile member were omitted.

Painters further south had recourse to a variety of artistic conventions in order to render human portraits. Sometimes, it was not only the features that were unrecognizable, but the whole body was conventionalized as well, as in the case of the match-stick or "filiform," men. More usually, the body was rendered in a seminaturalistic way but the head and face were given special treatment. The face might consist of a blob, as in Tassili, or it might be a blob surmounted by an inverted "U," a conventionalized form of head that puzzled Mr. Christie, Wood's friend, very much, and that convinced him that the paintings must represent some non-African race. Other conventions that deal with head problems, took the form of rendering it as a hook, or as an arrowhead.

Why did the rule of anonymity of faces extend to people who were presumably the enemies of the

Filoform men combine with strange symbols in this Matopos cave painting. (Photo Courtesy Rhodesian Ministry of Information.)

painters, such as the Bantu, and Whites, who were going to supplant them? One can only suppose that for most painters, faceless portraits had become so much the rule that they found it difficult to draw a picture with human features. Why, then, should portraits exist at all in which human features can be discerned and racial types at least guessed at? This could be one of the aberrant forms of painting that I mentioned earlier, or these individual portraits (for they are not very frequent) could be real magic pictures, portraits of enemies whom the artists drew on the wall of the cave and then shot with magic arrows — small pointless missiles that would leave no mark on the portrait, but that would, so the magician believed, inflict harm on the subject.

As will be seen, the attempt to discover racial types in the portraits, types who might have been the artists as well as the sitters, is fraught with difficulties. It is not merely that the profiles are wanting, in the great majority of cases, and that bodies are often conventionalized or mere silhouettes, but that there is a further difficulty in that the colors used are conventional. Elephants might be rendered in white, although they were certainly grey in real life, so that a figure with a pink face, such as the White Lady, need not really be portraits of white people. On the other hand, the painters sometimes did render racial types in their true colors, because figures recognizable like Bantu, by the shields and spears that they carry, or as Bushmen, are portrayed in black and red respectively.

Where a painting appears to carry real racial traits

is one well advised to put complete trust in what the painter has portrayed? The answere is "probably not." Owing to their inhibition against rendering faces the hunter-artists were not the best of por- traitists. Even the Europeans, who appear in the very latest frescoes and who undoubtedly seemed just as distinctively ugly to the Bushmen as the Bushmen did to them, are chiefly recognizable, not from their facial features because they are carrying guns, are mounted on horseback or in wagons, and are wearing hats. This consideration is a very important one because it suggests that there was some quality other than personal appearance that the artists were con- cerned with rendering. What could it have been? I shall try to answer that question later.

The races that could be expected to be found in an African rock painting are the following: Bushman, or Bushmanoid, a small delicately built man with very small hands and feet. One Bushwoman called Rachel, one of a band of murderers and cattle stealers who were such devoted retainers of the Bleek household, had such small feet that the outgrown boots of a child of eleven fitted her. The Bushman's color was yellow and his hair gathered in tiny peppercorn tufts on his head, so that he never had a complete head of hair, but preferred to wear a head covering of some sort, like his cousin the Hottentot. His profile was very distinctive, as the reader will see from the illustrations. I have not hesitated to dub it "monkey- like" because I want to emphasize that some of the faces in the Saharan paintings, which are referred to by other observers as "animal masks," are really

Strange forms, impossible to decipher, appear to the right of the "filiform" or matchstick men in this **painting from Matopos, Rhodesia. (Photo Courtesy of Rhodesian Ministry of Information.)**

These elephants on a Tanzanian cave may be wallowing in a swamp, or they may be enclosed in some kind of trap, with hunters closing in. (Photo Courtesy Ministry of National Education, Tanzania.)

Bantu drummers. (Painting by Helen Tongue. Photo by Stella Mayes Reed.)

A Hottentot. (Photo by Stella Mayes Reed.)

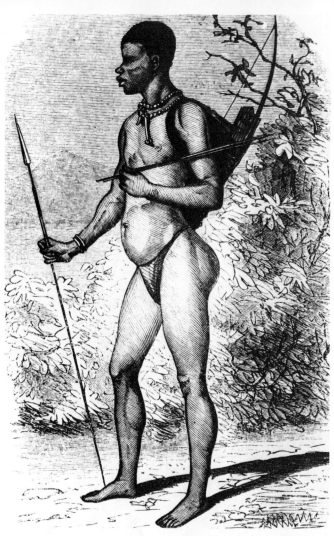

A Hottentot. From Wood. (Photo by Stella Mayes Reed.)

A Hottentot wearing a cap. Many headdresses appear in the paintings. (Photo by Stella Mayes Reed.)

A Hottentot girl. From Wood. (Photo by Stella Mayes Reed.)

Buck, men with blue jackets, and sheep, which must belong to the Hottentots. (Painting by Helen Tongue. Photo by Stella Mayes Reed.)

Bushman profiles. The lower spine of the Bushman curved forward somewhat, and, though Europeans were prepared to find this aesthetically pleasing in the Venus de Milo (who exhibits the same trait to a lesser extent), they found it odd in the Bushman. Another characteristic, much observed by white settlers in the Bushwomen and the Hottentots, was their fat buttocks, or "steatopygia." In fact, a kindly nature appears to have formed the Bushmen just for the environment they now inhabit, the pitiless sands of the Kalahari. The fat buttocks act as a reserve of energy, like the camel's hump, the eyes shielded by folds of skin seem a natural protection against the sand-laden winds of the desert.

Considerable controversy has arisen as to the position of the Bushmen virile member. Some observers claim that this is usually horizontal, while others dispute this. The female sexual organs also display a characteristic that is very striking and ought therefore to find representation in the rock paintings, though apparently it does not. This is the elongation of the *labia minora,* which early observers describe as hanging down and looking purple like the wattles of a turkey cock.

Racially, the Hottentots resembled the Bushmen very much. Were the early Hottentots tall men who degenerated in size through marrying Bushwomen? Some of the beachcombing or "strandloping" tribes of the coast are supposed to have arisen from crosses of this sort. Were they small, like the Bushman, and have they now increased their size through a better diet? Both points of view have been held.

The white men or Caucasoids of Africa belong to the same race as the Mediterranean people. They inhabit the northern parts of Africa even today, and they were also inhabiting East Africa before the arrival of the Negroids. Opinions would differ as to what constitutes a typical Caucasoid African race, but the Somalis would probably be considered to have many Caucasoid traits. They have a fair skin, and curly hair, which can grow quite long, as in the long hair styles affected by the ancient Egyptians, another Caucasoid race. They can grow a beard, and have straight or aquiline noses. The lips may be thick but are more often thin, giving the face what some consider a cruel expression, while the chin is firm.

The Negroid is a tall man with a figure that gives an impression of great strength (Bantu women can pick up loads of bushwood and place them on their head that a white man could not even lift from the ground). Often, the strength of the figure is emphasized by a barrellike chest and long arms. Negroids have a loping stride, bulging lips that turn out, flattish nose, and a high forehead. Unlike the average Negroid, the Bergdama of southwest Africa had massive eyebrow ridges. Negroids in South Africa, such as the Bantu, often pursued a policy of incorporation that left them with many traits of the subdued nations whom they brought into their political orbit. They sometimes exhibit marked intellectual foreheads.

Pygmoids who lived and still live in the central African forests were dwarfish, with a coffee-colored skin, a prognathous face, a bulging forehead, flattish nose, thick lips, and, occasionally, fat buttocks.

What about the Semites, who had been occasional visitors to Africa from the dawn of history and

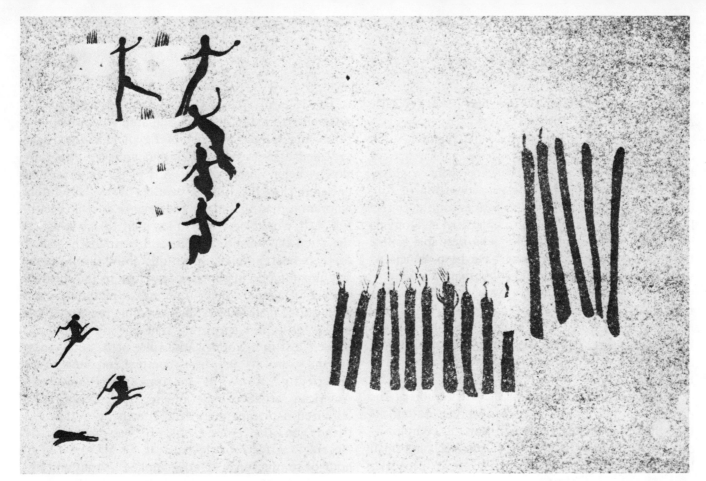

Basutos drumming on shields. Other figures stand by in karosses (fur cloaks or coats). (Painting by Helen Tongue. Photo by Stella Mayes Reed.)

settlers on the east coast from at least the seventh century? Though they had left their mark on Africa, as can be seen from the structure of the ancient Egyptian language, no one, save the Abbé Breuil, has claimed to discover Semitic types in the rock paintings.

With the exception of the Semites and the Pygmies, all the African races have been observed in the rock frescoes, but some are more frequent than others. Bushmanoids seem to be the most common, followed by Hottentots, Negroids, and Caucasoids (most of whom are very late arrivals in the form of Dutch and white settlers) with the Bergdama appearing only in South West Africa.

The task of piecing out bits of the racial jigsaw exhibited by the cave paintings has been made very difficult by various factors. The recognition of any racial trait in a painting is, in the end, a subjective matter. What appears "Cretan" to the Abbé Breuil in the White Lady (he also thought her "Egyptian"

Men putting on their shields with elands and red roe bucks. (Painting by Helen Tongue. Photo by Stella Mayes Reed.)

55

which is a very different thing) may seem typically African to Professor van Reit Lowe.

There is no doubt, moreover, that painters took considerable liberties with physical appearance of their subjects. Just as anyone who opens a glossy magazine will discover a higher proportion of full-breasted women than he is likely to encounter in real life, so the Painters of Tassili emphasized steatopygia because it was considered to be a desirable sexual trait, possibly because it may have been associated with fecundity in women. The "Aurignacian Venus" statues of prehistoric Europe were also idealized. A portrait of a man with a very long nose at Tassili may be the picture of a Semite, but it is much more likely to be a caricature. The rock painters of all schools had a marked sense of humor that constantly appeared in their work.

It is unfortunate as regards the attribution of the paintings either to the Bushmen or the Hottentots that they had so many physical traits in common — distinctive profiles, light skins, steatopygia, and small hands and feet. Though Alexander R. Willcox has argued very persuasively that the palm prints that occur on so many rock paintings are Bushman, because of their small size, the Hottentots also has small hands, and, in any case, there is no evidence that the hands portrayed were adult ones.

So the search for racial origins in the paintings tends to come up against a blank wall. All that can be said is that the cave artists differed in many ways from the races of Africa today. If they were Bushmen, they must have lengthened their hair by attaching fibres to it. They must also have been Bushmen of greater stature than those of today. Many paintings were either much idealized, or are very difficult to relate to present-day African types. The White Lady, for example, has a body eight times the height of her head, the same proportions as a modern European male.

As I shall try to suggest in a subsequent paragraph, the hunter artists were not content to portray life just as it was. They may have drawn idealized pictures of everyone they saw, just as we shall see their depiction of other aspects of life was by no means entirely governed by realism. Many of the pictures drawn by the hunter artists may therefore be of people as they would have liked to see them, not as they really were — just as the Mannerist artists in sixteenth-century Europe drew women with swan necks. I cannot help feeling that this applies particularly to the height of the male figures and their over emphasized virility.

The rules of art for the rock painters were totally different from the nearest comparable paintings, the tomb and temple frescoes of Egypt, and they have provided a series of puzzles that are even now only slowly being disentangled. A French observer has declared that the hunter painters were "absolutely ignorant of aesthetics or the science of the beautiful."[2] It would be truer to say that the rock artists shattered the universe to bits and remolded it nearer to their heart's desire. Since this desire was to paint the unpaintable, in approaching close to the spiritual essence of animals, men, trees, rocks, mountains, and even quite small objects such as edible roots or flying insects, it is not surprising that the observer finds himself lost in a world whose rules he can only guess at and can at the best comprehend only very imperfectly. He is in the same position as an American artist of the nineteenth century, who criticized a picture of a tiger, drawn by a Japanese friend, on the ground that it was anatomically incorrect. After looking hard at his picture for an hour or so, the Japanese artist replied: "Anatomically it *may* be incorrect, but morally it is perfect!"

Some of the artistic conventions of the rock painters, which seem so strange, have been noticed in passing. Color is unimportant; an ostrich may be blue, or black and blue, and black ostriches may appear in the same picture. A giraffe can be white, spotted with pink, while the foliage of the same tree can be rendered in dark brown, light brown, and black. Color was supremely irrelevant to the hunter painters, not merely because they were of course limited to the colors they had available, and because they never had a complete palette of colors they were debarred from ever rendering *anything* completely realistically, but because color is irrelevant to the spiritual essence of any being — what color is an angel or ought an angel to be?

For the same reason, the artists rejected perspective and foreshortening. There are examples of both of these devices in some of the paintings and they have been hailed as evidence of how the painters progressed and how they were developing their art to that pitch of perfection which, if it had ever been reached, would have presumably have included nothing but foreshortened figures set in perspective. To me, there seems no evidence that the few examples we have of perspective and foreshortening indicate anything other than a desire to experiment.

[2] Jean Dominique Lajoux, *Merveilles Du Tassili N-Ajjer*, p. 15.

They are examples of the aberrant styles to which I referred previously. There is no need for any spiritual being to be represented on the ground, or in perspective to any other creatures with whom he appears. Even medieval painters faced with this difficulty had to adopt all sorts of rather improbable conventional accompaniments for the saints. They appeared on clouds, though it is difficult to see why there should be clouds in heaven, and thus the problem of relating them to their background was solved. The rock painters simply depict everything as swimming in the void. The background is disregarded, and so, too, is the size of the figures. Instead of their assuming a relative proportion, this is disregarded and, instead, they are painted any size that the artist wants them to be.

It is the same story when it comes to rendering the outline of form or interior detail. Bushman painting is delightfully vague; it is this that gives it its enigmatic charm. A particular animal may be what it seems to be, but it might well be something else. Though the painters could paint in a delightfully realistic style, when they chose, the did not always choose to paint in this way. They had a sure eye for movement — a point made by a recent film about the Bushmen that contrasted pictures of jumping game on the rocks with stills of the same animals in flight, arrested halfway through a spring, yet they did not hesitate to depict animals in quite unnatural poses, such as floating about on their backs.

Even in the best-drawn game animals, such as the elands, there is a dreamlike quality. If one were to measure up one of these eland pictures with a ruler he would soon see that the animals have unnaturally elongated bodies. Observers who are committed to the view that the rock painters were faultless animal artists find it difficult to reconcile this view with, for example, an elephant with both tusks on one side of its head. They usually take refuge in the assertion that the badly drawn pictures are either early primitives or works of the decandence. Yet, it has always seemed to me that if there is one characteristic that marks rock art right through its history it is this air of unreality that hangs over it. Take just one example. A British cavalryman is taking part in an eland hunt in a picture from one of the Drakensberg sites, Bellevue, site 32. This must be one of the latest cave paintings ever to be made and it shows, around the outside of the cavalryman's black overalls, a red line. Alfred R. Willcox, with his usual enthusiasm for all things Bushmen, says that the details of the uniform were all observed and correctly painted.[3] Yet, it seems to me that the red stripe is the strip of braid that should run down the *middle* of the leg of the overalls, not the outside.

We are far from able to interpret all the artists' conventions. Why are there so many animal-headed men in the paintings? Was it because they are mythological beings, or is it just a convenient device to eliminate the human features, something that we remember, the painters were at pains to suppress?

No artistic convention of the artist has created greater problems for those who wish to interpret his work than his habit of overpainting, or as it is usually called "superposition." It is very rare to find any painted rock that does not contain at least one painting that has been overpainted. Some disappear in a palimpsest of overpaintings. That this was a convention, not a convenience, can be seen from the fact that round the overpainted pictures there are many blank surfaces that would have formed canvasses just as good for pictures but that have been neglected. It would have been just as easy for the painters to scrape off an old painting and start with a completely fresh surface as to paint on top of an old one, because the color underneath sometimes showed through and must have altered the artist's concept of the picture as he had it in his mind when he started work. Moreover, the work of scraping off an old painting to make room for a new one was minimal compared with the task of preparing the rock for a rock engraving — a task that the artist apparently undertook quite readily. This strange rule that old work must never be removed but overpainted is also observed in the cave paintings of prehistoric Europe. How did it originate? George William Stow has this to say on the subject: "At a rock shelter on the banks of the Imvani, in the Queenstown division, as many as five distinct series of paintings were found, one over the other. The old Bushmen assert that the productions of an artist were always respected as long as any recollection of him was preserved in his tribe; during this period no one, however daring, would attempt to deface his paintings by placing others over them. But when his memory was forgotten, some aspirant after artistic fame appropriated the limited rock surface of the shelter adapted for such a display of talent for his own performances, and unceremoniously painted over the efforts of those who preceded him. If we calculate that the memory of an artist

[3] Willcox, *Drakensberg,* Plate 47.

would be preserved for at least three generations . . . it would give a probable antiquity of about five hundred years to the oldest found in the Imvani rock shelter."[4]

It seems very unlikely that such an anarchical people as the Bushmen should observe such a rigid rule of art. Nowadays, the person most likely to overpaint a picture would be the artist himself. Artists often have an overmodest regard for their own work. Some of it they destroy and some of it changes while still in the studio. I shall try to suggest elsewhere that since the purpose of the paintings was religious, the spiritual or magical force implanted in the new paintings was enhanced by the existence of older ones. After I had adopted this idea I was glad to see that it had been already entertained by Sonia Cole, who stressed that certain sites that were frequented over long periods by painters might have acquired magical or religious significance.[5] The idea of the old regenerating the new is one of great antiquity in Africa. The ancient Egyptians carefully selected stones from old or ruined temples that would be built into new ones. Even nowadays one of the difficulties about acquiring fragments of old manuscripts or icons from Coptic monasteries in Egypt is that all old church accessories are conserved in special lumber rooms. From here, they are withdrawn from time to time to serve as fuel for the fire that heats up the chrysm used in church ceremonies. The monks believe that the holiness of the old objects is imparted to the newly made chrysm.

Whatever the purpose of the overpainting, its effect has been to render much more difficult the task of interpreting the paintings that have been affected in this way. One of the most famous Tassili paintings is covered with small overpainted figures. Have these been added later, or are they part of the original composition? It is impossible to tell. Obviously, overpainting has increased the ambiguity of the art, an art already so ambiguous that what seems a young lady to a French abbé seems a North African visitor to a South African photographer.

The attempts made by archaeologists to use overpainting paintings as an aid to establishing a sequence in the paintings have often complicated the issue

rather than rendering it more clear. Obviously, in a rock shelter, matchstick figures in brown that overlay naturalistic elands, well rendered in claret paint, which, in turn, cover yellow elephants painted rather crudely and demonstrate the elands, came last, but they do not establish whether the elands came last by a month or so, or perhaps by several thousand years.

The problems of developing overpaintings into a sequence were even more considerable than this example suggests, however. When Frobenius and Breuil confidently put forward a sequence of no fewer than sixteen color phases for the Orange Free State in South Africa, periods of artistic development there that had been characterized by the use of a different color or group of colors, in the manner of Picasso's "Blue Period," other workers in the field challenged this idea. They admitted that they were prepared to point to particular paintings that they felt to be early, middle, or late in date, but that this was because of differences in subject or style, certainly not because they were painted in one particular color, much less because they were overlaid by pictures of another color. Overpaintings often turned up in unexpected order, these observers pointed out, and why should they not, seeing that artists may be short of a particular color but seize the nearest pigment to hand — just as G.K. Chesterton did when he broke off a piece of the Downs (which are made of chalk) on which he was sketching, to complete his pastel sketch. Identical colors or groups

At least two sets of painters have been at work in Mlanda Cave, one of whom drew schematic paintings, the other much larger paintings that may represent filiform men. (Photo Courtesy Malawi Tourist Agency.)

[4] George William Stow, *The Native Races of South Africa*, quoted in Dorothea F. Bleek, *Rock Paintings in South Africa*, p. 18.

[5] Sonia Cole, *The Prehistory of East Africa* (London: Weidenfeld and Nicholson, 1964).

of colors could be used by artists of all periods. Furthermore, as I have already noticed, overpainting can merge, or even obliterate, the layer of paint underneath, making disentanglement well-nigh impossible. So superposition sequences, which once seemed so hopeful, have now been largely abandoned, and sequences are now worked out much more in terms of style. Another of the many hopeful-looking avenues in rock painting has turned out to be a blind alley.

The purely abstract, conventionalized, or schematic designs that cover so many rock surfaces, and that mingle even with the realistic paintings so that dots and dashes are combined with representational paintings, have surely caused more difficulties to interpreters than any other aspect of the rock pictures.

Daringly, archaeologists have striven to recognize natural or man-made objects in some of the abstract designs, some of the more stereotyped of which have special names such as "formlings." These interpretations are often very plausible. Elizabeth Goodall has identified oval-shaped elements in paintings from Mashonaamd as rocks and landscapes.[6] I grasped eagerly at this solution as a possible clue leading out of the maze of schematic paintings. However, a little further on, Mrs. Goodall's "rocks" have apparently become transparent, because figures can be seen through them,[7] while elsewhere the rocks have become a "rock motive." A little later in the same publication in which Mrs. Goodall's interpretations appear, C.K. Cooke, her co-author, commenting on an oblong, very similar in style and shape to those which Mrs. Goodall has tried to interpret, dismisses it as "a tectiform composition for which I can give no satisfactory explanation, although rocks, grain bins, African xylophones and quivers have all been suggested." Of another composition, he says, with commendable restraint, "This has been interpreted as a honey collecting scene and also as the shelter itself with Matopo Hills above and skins hanging down in front of it. It could be almost anything."[8]

The grid patterns of rock art have been interpreted as being game nets or snares, the dots and dashes as tallies. When we come to mythological interpretations we will see that these dots, which are, as Stow

remarked "the mystery of these paintings," will do duty as drops of blood, or as raindrops from a rain animal.

Difficulties in determining the meaning of paintings run through the whole of rock art. Though some scenes are readily enough understood, others are completely baffling. This bafflement is strongest in the abstract paintings, but it is not confined to them. French archaeologists have argued rather acidly whether scenes in the Tassili frescoes represent the sale of a young girl, whether spots on a figure are ornaments, or symptoms of a painful disease. They have also (I feel wisely) declined to interpret scenes that, to my mind at least, have definite sexual interpretations. More often than declining to guess, observers have sought solutions that are rather improbable, taking refuge in the explanation that it is a "ceremony" or in the mythological interpretation, which will be discussed in a moment. Whether the symbols or the ambiguous figures had some specific meaning for the artists, as for example the picture of an egg had for Picasso when he decided to express God the Father by this figure, is difficult to tell. What can be said without any fear of contradiction is that the pictures, as they stand, convey that air of mystery which is one of the chief characteristics of life and they are, therefore, very illustrative of the idea behind the object that the painters were so eager to convey.

The mythological interpretations of the paintings were initially conceived by Stow, but it is unlikely that Stow would have thought of them for himself — more likely they were suggested to him by his Bushmen helpers. Here, we come up against what is undoubtedly the greatest of all the problems connected with rock paintings, the fact that we are dealing with a broken tradition. Any attempt to pick up from where the now extinct rock painters left off is going to be as difficult as getting back to the native art of Easter Island now that the island tradition has been severed by the "blackbirders" who carried off so many of the islanders to work as slave labor in the guano diggings. The break with the Bushmen and their art has been felt more strongly than in any comparable situation. The only valid comparison is Tasmania, where again the aborigines were exterminated before they could convey the secret traditions of their art to posterity. Other parts of the world have been more favored. The art of the Eskimo, for example, is often puzzling and obscure, but there are still Eskimo artists at work who can be observed

[6]Goodall, Cooke, and Clark, *Prehistoric Rock Art of the Federation of Rhodesia and Nyasaland*, p. 16.

[7]Ibid., p. 64-65.

[8]Ibid., p. 145.

carrying out their art and interrogated about their motivation.

No white man ever talked to a real Bushman painter about his work, so our knowledge of painting methods is largely speculative, and our knowledge of the motivation dependent on the scattered remnant of the Bushman nation, men and women who had suffered a complete culture shock, and who were still reeling under the brutal attacks inflicted on them by white and black alike. These disturbed and unhappy people who found a brief, insecure refuge in the Bleek household before being called in other directions by family loyalties, were certainly not the best interpreters of what must have been a very complicated mythology and folklore.

What sort of an account of Roman mythology would be given by two Roman criminals who had been enslaved by the Parthians? The whole edifice of Bushman mythology is certainly there in Bleek's notebooks, but how much of it was invented to amuse a kindly master?

It is the same story, to my mind, with Stow's Bushmen interpreters of his copies of Bushman paintings. His Bushmen friends wanted to help, and they were prepared to say something that they felt would fill the vacuum in Stow's mind. They were none of them painters, the only persons who really knew what the paintings were really about, just as nowadays an artist is the only true interpreter of his paintings. Two of Stow's helpers were quite elderly, seventy and eighty, in a race that, as Wood put it, grows old at twenty-six.

At all events, the interpretations given by the Bush folk to the Warwickshire man do not carry conviction, or not complete conviction. The only pictures that they were prepared to interpret at all were the ones at which we could all of us have tried our hands. They left the really baffling paintings completely alone.

Here are a few of the Bushmens' interpretations of Stow's copies. The reader can judge for himself whether I am being unkind to them. When shown a group of men with one leg raised and the arms held akimbo, one Bushman remarked, "They seem to be dancing." They took figures to be female that have, to my eye at least, no female characteristic.[9] They interpreted as "a Boer Commando," a group of horsemen, only one of whom carries a gun.[10] Even

Dorothea Bleek, Stow's editor, who had a great regard for Stow and a wide experience with Bushmen, found one of the Bushman interpretations "incomprehensible." This was the comment made on a painting of some twenty-three people, who are accompanied by a large number of shield-shaped objects. "Lion to the right. His daughter in white close to it. The lion on the other side belongs to the other lot of people." Here again I found it impossible to find a single female figure.

Other explanations seemed even more incomprehensible. One of them referred to a picture of a monstrous animal as, "The rain with white quartz which has hail."[11] Stow's informants gave accounts of some pictures that seemed at variance with their interpretation of other similar pictures, with the little we do know about the Bushmen, and even with common sense.

One Bushman, when shown a picture of animal-headed beings, said, "They put on this dress because they want to see whether we shall laugh at them."[12] One wonders whether it were not the Bushmen who were occasionally laughing at Stow — they were very fond of a joke. Crouching figures covered with eland skins were interpreted as "People killed by lightning,"[13] in one picture, while in another painting which was not very different they were a "Dance of men and women."

One fact did emerge from the many questions that Stow put to them on the subject of the paintings. They could refer to individual parts of the paintings by their colors, thus disposing, I feel, of Alexander R. Willcox's contention that they were partly color blind. People of ready wit and of a childlike imagination, the Bushmen were ready to produce their own explanation for everything that was puzzling. When one of them encountered Miss Bleek's rocking horse, for example, he immediately found a name for it: "goin goin." In the same way, I would suggest, Stow and Bleek's informants were equally ready to supply an answer to any problem with which they were faced.

When pressed to interpret anything that seemed very complex, these informants took refuge in mythology. Animal-headed figures, when not interpreted as men out hunting in animal disguises, were referred to as subjects in the very extended animal

[9] Bleek, *Rock Paintings in South Africa*, Plate 7.
[10] Ibid., Plate 8.

[11] Ibid., Plate 42.
[12] Ibid., Plate 16.
[13] See Ibid., Plate 21, and Willcox *Drakensberg*, pp. 55-56.

pantheon of the Bushmen. Any grotesque and unearthly animal was a "rain animal."

The attempt to identify difficult subjects as part of Bushman mythology has been taken up by white observers like Stow and, much more recently, the late Francis Klingender. Both felt that they could interpret a painting in terms of the "nose bleeding dance," a Bushman ceremonial.

"The most famous dance among Bushmen," remarks Stow "was that called Mo'koma, or the dance of blood . . . . It is a circular dance of men and women following each other, and it is danced all night. Some fall down, some become as if mad and sick; blood runs from the noses of others . . . . When a man thus falls, the women gather round him and put two bits of reed across each other on his back."[14] Whereas, however, the plate chosen by Stow as an illustration of this dance shows blob-headed women bowing to one another on one side of the drawing while beast-headed men brandish knobkerries on the other and one beast headed man appears to be carrying off a blob-headed woman on his back. Over his shoulder hang traces attached to which is the prostrate body of a blob-headed man with an infibulated member, which he drags behind him. Stow's interpretation of this scene was that the drag lines were reeds, the left-hand side of the picture represented women performing the Mo'koma dance, while on the right Kaggen, the Mantis demigod of the Bushmen, was beating a sinner with a digging stick.

Such was the scene and such Stow's interpretation of it. Francis Klingender, on the other hand, saw his picture of the dance in a group of three animal-headed figures from Teyateyaneng in Lesotho. Of the group, two bend over the third, while long broken lines like the dashes in Morse code hang from their muzzles. A third figure with a protuberance that might be either an outflung hand or a breast, holds what appears to be a spear. Klingender's caption for this picture was as follows. "Men with Animal Heads and noses bleeding, watched by a woman." The broken lines could signify drops of blood, but they could also represent practically anything else that one would care to think of. Alexander R. Willcox, faced with a spotted animal from Giant's Castle Game Reserve, Natal, whose muzzle also emits broken lines, does not hesitate to suggest that it is "perhaps spitting forth rain." I shall show myself equally daring

in my hypotheses and suggest that the dots and dashes that are so common in rock painting represent the quality that the artists were determined to inject into their paintings but that they could not paint realistically because it is invisible, namely the spiritual life force that pervades all beings, and that to the Bushmen also pervaded inanimate objects and even tools and weapons as well. Here again, we can find analogies in medieval art. A medieval artist, faced with the task of representing the soul, might well paint it as a small, circular, luminous disk that issued from the mouth of a man on his death. The Emperor Frederick II, it will be remembered, was so keen to investigate the existence of this "visible" soul that he even had a prisoner executed in a hermetically sealed barrel and then searched for the soul.

If all rock paintings are religious in origin, as I shall try to prove, is it possible to refer to any specific ones that do display mythological beings? The argument that can be applied to totemism holds good here with regard to mythology as well. If some of the paintings are about totemism or mythology, why is it that the creatures that we hear most about in Bushman folklore, and that presumably had a large part to play as totems as well, do not appear in them? These creatures do appear, here and there, but they play a very secondary role, and it is legitimate to speculate that, if any of the paintings were mythological, we should see a lot of the Mantis, that creature who had as much to do in Bushman mythology as did Brer Rabbit in mythology of a rather similar sort.

Though it is always easy to be wise after an event, it is still permissible to criticize Stow and Bleek for setting about matters in the wrong way. Instead of merely encouraging their Bushmen helpers to interpret existing paintings for them, what they should have done was to have given them a pencil or a paint box (Stow's apprentice could paint very well) and tell them to paint all the creatures of the legends. Then we might have known something about the iconography of Bushman folklore. At it is, it is difficult not to assume that we have not one, but several perhaps contradictory accounts of what mythological creatures looked like. Take the work of Orpen, for example. In 1874, Orpen reproduced details of some Bushmen paintings in the Maluti Mountains and accompanied them by eight legends told him by a young Bushman, a last survivor of the tribe of Maluti Bushmen who had been exterminated very recently. Qing, his informant (one of the few Bushmen to give their real names, unlike some even of Bleek's pro-

[14]Ibid., Plate 71.

tégés), did explain the pictures to him, and pointed out that the dashes that issued from the mouths of the animal-headed characters in the paintings represented drops of blood shed during a dance. Qing's information may have been perfectly authentic, yet it may have differed from that given by, say, Stow's helpers. Just as there was more than one Bushman language, and as Alexander R. Willcox has suggested more than one Bushman mythology, so there might well be more than one system of iconography.

3

The Technique of Art

Much may be conjectured, but little is known for certain about the techniques employed by the rock artists in making paintings and engravings. "Whence they obtained their colors," wrote Macdonald, a contemporary of the last Bushmen, or with what ingredients they mixed them, no one knows." The art, rude as it was, has been lost and many eminent men have puzzled over the secret in vain. Though great efforts have been made to reconstitute the Bushman palette, efforts attended with a great deal of success, it has been more a question of collecting the pieces of the jigsaw together rather than putting them in place. Only when the colors of the reconstituted pigments, which are claimed to closely resemble those of the Bushmen, have been put to the test of exposure to the sun for many years will it be really possible to answer the question of whether the secret of the lost Bushman paintings has been rediscovered or not.

Meanwhile, all is conjecture. One of the biggest advances that has been made in the study of rock art has been the discovery, by Dr. Denninger, that the early paintings were made with pigment, mixed with animal fat as a binder or fixative. There is very little doubt that this was done, because early travelers attest the use of animal fat for just this purpose.

Its presence in the early pigments is not proof that it was included as a binder. However, it may have

Rock engravings were pecked or incised by means of stone tools, such as these examples from Zambia. (Photo Courtesy Zambian Tourist Board.)

63

gotten mixed in accidentally. The Bushman, that representative of earlier painters, was a man of very Bohemian habits in eating and cooking. What could be more likely than that he should have mixed his paints in the nearest vessel available, a cooking pot? So, even this apparently stable ground need not prove certain.

Let us look first at the paintings, not merely because there are many more of them than the engravings, but because they illustrate a much wider field of subjects, and because, in them, the genius of the rock artist rises to its greatest heights. It cannot be accidental that the rock painters did what the ancient Egyptians boasted that they too were able to do, create colors that would last forever. This can only be the result of a long apprenticeship to the art, a period of trial and error that was crowned, at last, by success.

Possibly, the painters started by experimenting with crayons, pyramid-shaped blocks of natural color that are still to be found in the caves. Crayons continued to be used for roughing out subjects, but because the painters noticed that the color they left was only surface deep, and did not penetrate below the skin of the rock as did grease-based color, they abandoned crayons in favor of mixed paint for their most important work. These paintings can still be seen under infrared light, at Tassili N Ajjer, and even in Rhodesia or South Africa. Though the pigment has rubbed off the surface, the colors have sunk deep into the rock, thanks to the vehicle that was used to bind them.

Have any rock paintings, other than those at Tassili faded away? Some faded specimens have been restored under infrared light in Central Africa, but one wonders whether they faded or whether they were not simply rubbed off the surface of the rock by animals such as penned cattle, for example. Stow was convinced that paintings faded, but that was what he wished to believe because it bolstered his conviction that the paintings could not be very old. Other observers, such as Alexander R. Willcox, have argued that paintings do not fade. Those which were observed by former students of the art are still to be seen, as bright as ever.

It is possible to suggest what kind of paintings would be most in hazard, and least likely to survive to this day. Those near a road, those in shelters deep enough to pen cattle or to invite wayfarers to light a fire, or to take refuge there. Caves are natural cities

of refuge for Africans and even the smallest shelter could provide a home at a pinch. I noted with surprise just how small some of the shelters were that accommodated Malawian fugitives from the slave traders or the Ngoni when I was examining rock shelters on the Lengwe. Paintings made on flat, horizontal stones not protected by an overhang were obviously very much in hazard.

As has been already noticed, only some of the flat surfaces that might attract a painter seem to have been used. I shall endeavor to prove that these painted sites were selected for their sanctity. They were shrines, such as the Ti Bedjadi, in the Sahara, where naked feet are engraved on the rock and where the Touareg come to pour out milk and melted butter on the rocky surface as a sign of offering. When the Touareg are asked why they sacrifice to the engraved feet they just shrug their shoulders. They do not know the reason but carry out the custom, just as their ancestors did.

Many of the Bantu were more definite about their purpose in making offerings at caves. Willcox mentions sacred caves at Domboshawa in Rhodesia, in Transvaal, Transkei, Pondoland, and Soutpansberg in South Africa, where the Bantu propitiated the Bushmen who lived in the caves by giving them offerings of food so that they could make rain for them.

So the choice of a painting surface was not primarily artistic at all but religious. It is obviously for this reason that the Bushmen, now confined to the Kalahari, and apparently representative of different tribes than those who were exterminated in the Drakensberg and elsewhere, have refused to paint at all. There are no caves, so there can be no shrines.

There are several practical considerations that govern the location even of shrines, however. They must not be too far from the mainstream of life. Otherwise, they would attract no worshippers. Painted caves are located near to rivers that cut their way thorugh the mountains. Water may have been necessary for sacrifice; it was certainly necessary for the painters who "consecrated" the shrine by painting it, and for anyone who came to worship and offer sacrifice. The sites chosen also had a close proximity to the game grounds. The livelihood of the worshippers was, after all, confined to hunting, and worship cannot be carried out unless the worshipper is able to earn a living. Sterile and barren to modern eyes, the kloofs of the Drakensberg afforded a rich variety of

Paintings on walls (parietal art) took the place, among the Bantu, of cave paintings (rupestral art). *Photo by Stella Mayes Reed.*

Baboons. *Helen Tongue painting. Photo by Stella Mayes Reed.*

A puzzling—yet compelling—subject from a Rhodesian cave. *Photo courtesy of the Rhodesian Information Service.*

Ceremonial Scene, Rhodesia. *Photo courtesy of Rhodesian Information Service.*

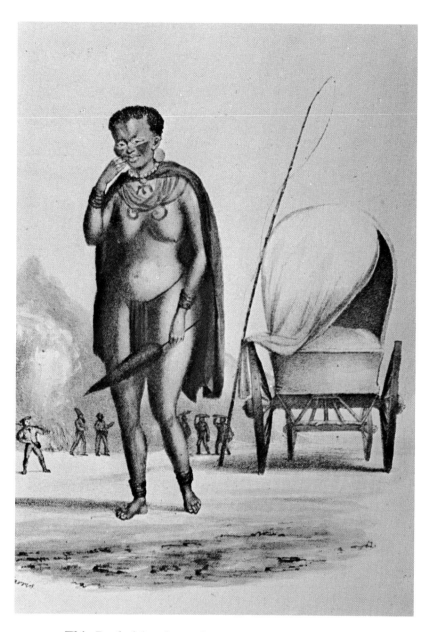

This Bushgirl, who seduced Harris' guards so that her relatives could steal his oxen, shows the slight form and incipient steatopygia of the Bushfolk. *Photo by Stella Mayes Reed.*

A painted rock shelter, Malawi. *Photo courtesy of the Malawi Tourist Board.*

'Mantis Man,' and schematic paintings, Chincherere Hill, Malawi. *Photo by William Pawek.*

These figures of elephants, zebra, rhino, and other game were superimposed on the figure of a gigantic elephant in this painting from the Manemba Cave, Mtoko District of Rhodesia. Did months, or millenia, intervene between the two sets of paintings? (Photo Courtesy Rhodesian National Tourist Board.)

animals on which even nowadays a Bushman could subsist. It would also be possible for the artist hunters who set up the shrine to live a normal life while they undertook their task of painting, because it has been estimated that even today, in the Kalahari, the Bushmen spend three days out of their week hunting and the remainder doing nothing.

It is the rock formations of Africa that determine the distribution of the paintings. Where there are no crags and no caves there are no frescoes either. Hence some districts are completely barren of art, such as the sand belt that stretches from Malope to Rhodesia and that includes the Kalahari, where the remnants of the Bushmen now live. Here, no paintings are to be found, but in the other, craggy parts of Africa, such as the Tassili, rock paintings abound.

The larger the mountains the more likely they are to contain caves and canyons, or *kloofs* as they are called in South Africa, *krans*, ridges of overhanging rock, and caves. Caves and kloofs figure largely in Bushman mythology. Indeed a cave is the womb of creation.

Though painters sought the same kind of territory all over Africa, they had local preferences for special kinds of rocks and settings. In Rhodesia, for example, one typical site is a rock shelter formed by sub-spheroidal weathering in which the rock has been

65

sculpted away, by weather, to form a smooth, excavated semicircle like the apse of a church. Another typical site is a slotted cave, one in which a slab of granite has split away from its parent bed of rock. Of all surfaces, granite was easily the most preferred in Rhodesia.

For the sake of completeness, let us glance just for a moment at the sites chosen for engravings. These were placed, not in caves but for the most part on tall outstanding knobs of rock called *Kopjes* or *Koppies.* From these rock towers, the artist hunters had wonderful views of the movements of the game. Here, because the rock did not provide large open surfaces protected by overhangs, the artists preferred to engrave rather than paint. Were the engraving sites shrines as well? At least one of them, as has been seen, still receives regular sacrifices even in the twentieth century, so it is possible that they, too, had religious significance.

Whereas the engravers chose for preference rock surfaces that were either naturally dark, such as sombre colored sandstone limestone or basalt, or some stone, such as dolerite, that had been covered with a darker layer of weathering, but were prepared at a pinch to put up with light-colored rocks such as granite or gniess, painters were much more selective. They specialized in light-colored stone canvasses such as white unoxidized sandstone and light brown granite.

The hypothesis of a religious nature for the rock paintings solves the very difficult question of why they should be painted on rock at all. There were many difficulties connected wih rock painting. To the modern eye, an unprepared and unprimed rock surface might seem to be, of all surfaces, the least promising. The rock painters must have possessed surfaces that were easier to paint on such as bone (used for occasional paintings by the Kalahari Bushmen), bark, and skin. Moreover painting in the rock shelters involved transporting oneself, and painting equipment, including a heavy ostrich shell container of liquified fat, up a hill.

In retrospect it may seem miraculous that any paintings have survived at all. The only respite they have received from being scorched by the African sun is the frosts of the night hours and the lash of the seasonal rains. Rock paintings are not cave paintings of the European sort, well protected by a long, tunnellike approach; they are shelter paintings set very close to the open sky. The shelters in which they are to be found have sunny aspects, perhaps so that the colors of the paintings will show up well. In spite of all the hazards of the weather, the paintings have survived, and they have endured all sorts of additional bad handling as well. The many buckets of water poured over them by photographers and sightseers have not dimmed their colors, or at least not appreciably so, while even the efforts of an iconoclastic schoolteacher who instructed her class to scrub off the "pagan" paintings in one cave, using brushes and water, merely brought up the hues of the painting.

Obviously the technology that could produce lasting frescoes of this sort was not to be despised. History is full of stories of unsuccessful fresco painters. Leonardo da Vinci, the greatest fresco painter the. world has ever seen, is memorable for two works, one of which, the *Battle of the Standard,* flaked from the walls of the Council Chamber at Florence almost as soon as it was put up, so that it had to be covered up by another painting some fifty years later, the other, the famous *Last Supper,* was only saved from complete disintegration by the restorer Cavaliere Cavenaghi.

Why did the artists succeed where the master of the renaissance failed? I have already said that we shall never know the whole truth, but it is possible to speculate about at least part of it. The Bushmen, and no doubt the earlier painters, from whom they inherited their technical skills, were accomplished chemists. The preparation of the arrow poison, and the other poisons used by the Bushmen in hunting, were extremely complicated processes compared to which the manufacture of paint was probably child's play.

One reason that the rock artists colors have lasted is that they were all natural ones. Some of the longest lived painters' colors in history, such as the Chinese red, made from coral, and the lapis lazuli blue and malachite green used by Chinese painters, have been natural, too. The artists were not content to use colors just as they found them in their natural state. However, they heated them and thus induced a color change.

The palette of the painters consisted of either mineral or vegetable materials. Plants were squeezed so that they could provide juices and sap for some paints – a procedure that the Bushmen, at least, were well used to in the preparation of arrow poison, where the juice of a particular poison bulb had to be extracted.

Red was probably obtained from the juice of the

Elands boontje (Elephantorrhiza burchellii), which, as its name implies, would commonly grow in hunting country frequented by elands, one of the principal game beasts of the hunters. Another plant, a species of *vellozia* that grew luxuriantly among the granite crags that were often the setting for the paintings, produced a pink pigment when it was burned and reduced to ashes. Various red berries, still used by Hottentot girls to paint their faces, were employed to give red. Mention will be made later on of *sibilo,* a red body paint employed by both Hottentots and Bushmen. Though it does not seem to have been recorded by any of the investigators of the paintings, there is every likelihood that it, too, was used as a pigment.

Berries and plants that could be chewed and carried in the mouth could then be sprayed from the artist's mouth right onto the rock, and this technique was apparently used to cover some of the hands that provided the stencil for the negative handprints painted on some shelter walls. As early travelers talk about Hottentot women amputating finger joints if they lost a husband, the absence of mutilated hands in these hand paintings probably proves that the painters were all men.

Chemical analysis by Dr. Denninger has now established that blood was also used as a pigment. Bushmen frequently killed animals by cutting their throat and then applying a tourniquet so that they bled inwardly and the blood could be collected and removed from the stomach. Fresh blood leaves a brownish stain and has an astonishingly lasting effect. The blood of David Rizzio, murdered by the Earls of Morton and Lindsay in 1566, could still be seen on the floor of Holyrood House, in Edinburgh, as late as the 1940s. It would still be there today if tourists had not removed it splinter by splinter from the floor as souvenirs.

Not only could fresh blood be used as a pigment, it could be induced to clot by whisking a twig in it and the residual clear serum used as a binder or fixative for paint.

Apart from the paints that have been mentioned and others that we do not know about, the most important pigments were mineral ones. Charcoal was used for preliminary sketching, just as it is today, and it was also used as a black paint. Most of the dating of cave paintings by radio carbon tests have been made from the black painted areas.

Rather late in the history of the Bushmen a tribesman called Silayi told a white inquirer that the raw material for painting was dug out of the ground

and treated in the fire. It would not be necessary to dig far in many areas of rock painting. Some of the ground surrounding rock sites in the Sahara is literally carpeted with red ochre. Heating, by driving out the water from some colors, would change them.

Other pigments were even to be found in the rock shelters themselves, present on the rock wall in the shape of the soft, earthy iron ore called limonite, a yellow ochre that is a natural excrescence or concretion on cave roofs. Limonite could be changed in color by heating it, and the assumption is that this discovery was made accidentally, when blocks of limonite (or haematite, which has the same property) built around a fire changed color because of the heat.

Though the rock painters, no doubt, did break down limonite into orange, umber, claret, and black, they could find natural limonite in at least three colors, black, yellow, and umber. Haematite occurred ready-packed for the painter, as it were, in nodules that could be easily broken in two and that contained the mineral in ready powdered form. During the nineteenth century, these were referred to as "Bushman's paint pots." The color haematite gave, red ochre, was not merely very important from the point of view of the palette, but it also had strong associations for prehistoric man, both in Africa and Europe. It was frequently used in burials and there is some suggestion that it was regarded as the color of life. It is not surprising, then, that so many paintings – the majority probably – were executed in some form of red, because, as I shall try to prove, the painters were essentially concerned with portraying the life force of beings as shown through their spiritual qualities.

White stalactite deposits may also have been used as a white pigment. Mr. Christie, in 1874, suggests that some parts of a painting in a cave situated in a kranz on the north side of the Zwart Ruggens were either natural excretions of stalactite, or areas of white paint made up from stalactites. Kaolin was another white paint, widely used in East Africa, and often applied very thickly.

The black of the pictures was either charcoal, manganese ore, which gave purple and purplish black, converted limonite, or burnt bone, which gave just as good a black as its modern counterpart, ivory black. It is fascinating to note that the other body paint used by Hottentots and Bushmen, specular iron, was also used as a black. It was stored in powder form in earthenware pots. It is quite possible, then, that rock painting may have been connected with body painting and that the paintings in the shelters may have had their counterpart in paintings on the bodies of the worshippers.

Other iron oxides produced colors ranging through brown red and purple to yellow. Oxidized yellow shale produced a yellow pigment, while schists with iron inclusions gave various colors. Besides kaolin, gypsum, clay, and lime, deposits produced white, and bird droppings, either fresh or in the shape of guano — a fertilizer often found in the caves that has led to the discovery of many new sites by farmers who were searching for it — produced white. Fresh bird droppings sometimes ate away at the surface of the rock, and then dropped off, leaving a white silhouette that gives an impression of great antiquity.

Thus, the palette of the rock painters was a very extensive one, though it did not include every color that would be found in a modern paintbox, a fact that may have had something to do with abandoning naturalism in favor of impressionism.

Red ochre was, as has been said, the preferred color, the one that provides so many of the monochrome paintings, which are sometimes painted, sometimes drawn directly onto the rock with a crayon. Most of the colors we have noticed allowed themselves to be formed into crayons. Variants of red such as claret, light red, pink, maroon, and dark brown red, together with black, were also popular for monochromes, as was black with its derived colors grey and off-white. White, yellow, and orange were popular, but blue was very uncommon.

The secret of the durability and unfading nature of the rock painters' pigments undoubtedly lay in the fixative that was mixed with them rather than the paints themselves. The widest conjectures have been made to ascertain what the binders might have been. Probably quite a number were in use at one time or another, because, while Dr. Pietsch has confirmed the use of casein products as a fixative in the Sahara, Dr. Denninger has discovered that blood — probably in the shape of blood serum — was used in the Southern African paintings. Other suggestions, some of them a little improbable, have been put forward. They include plant saps, tree gums, animal fat, white of ostrich egg or whole ostrich egg, and the urine of the hyrax or rock rabbit.

Tree sap, in the form of the juice of a species of sumach, is used for the basis of that other imperishable paint, lacquer. Was it employed as a binder for rock paintings as well? Tallow or melted grease have

been suggested as likely binders and they are both probable suggestions because they have been confirmed by Denninger's analysis and they are also mentioned by early travelers.

It has been objected that the paint used by the rock painters was very liquid — drops of it have splashed onto the ground below the frescoes. There is a distinct possibility that ostrich fat and marrow, which stay liquid once they have melted, were used. I would like to suggest a much simpler binder that no one has yet suggested, melted butter. As everyone knows, butter, once it has been melted, does not resolidify readily, least of all in the burning African sun. Many of the paintings represent long-tailed sheep, suggesting that some, at least, of the artists were shepherds, like the Hottentots, who also kept cattle. Cattle appear widely in the Sahara, and, of course, they were kept by the men of Tassili as domestic animals. Whether they were ever used by the rock painters further south, except as spoils taken from herdsmen of other tribes, is somewhat in dispute. Even Bushmen, though, could have used the milk from animals that they had killed to make butter.

Perhaps the most mysterious binder is rock rabbit urine. Though, like everyone who has ever visited Africa, I have seen rock rabbits, I have never come across their solidified urine, which is described as a black, sticky mass, like tar, clinging to the walls of caves and difficult to remove. It is difficult to see just how a black substance of this sort could either be liquefied or used as a binder for light colors. Nevertheless, it did enter into the Bushman compendium of materials, because it is almost certainly the black sticky substance that Harris describes the little people using to add to their arrow poison.

Johnson, Rabinowitz, and Sieff, the indefatigable team of researchers who tried to reconstitute the lost rock artist pigments felt that, of all the media with which they experimented for use as binder, egg tempera was the best. Egg tempera was certainly the medium that has preserved those other marvelously bright African paintings, the icons of Coptic Nubia and Egypt, and the illuminations of the medieval manuscripts of Ethiopia.

Objections have been raised to the use of egg tempera on the ground that there was only one likely source for it, the egg of the ostrich, and that this could not have been used as a binder for pigment because it formed too important an addition to the food of the group. This objection could equally well be raised to blood or fat, however, and both of these were used. Moreover, although an ostrich egg never got too bad for a Bushman to eat, Bushmen traveled in small groups while ostriches laid their eggs in a large clump. There can be little doubt that the Bushmen occasionally found more eggs than they could eat or carry around. They hated to carry burdens, and one way of using the eggs would be to mix them up as binder.

Ingenious in their choice and treatment of pigments, the painter showed at least an equal skill in the manner in which they applied them. The colored earths and mineral ores that were the base for the pigments were ground down to a fine powder on a stone slab with a slabber. Many examples of slabs and slabbers have been recovered from the rock shelters, some of which are still stained red from the pigment — though there is, of course, no evidence that the color they produced was meant for wall paintings rather than for the adornment of the body.

Other pieces of ore were ground into a crayon shape, which was either pyramid-shaped or round. These crayons were used to apply color direct or, more usually, to sketch in outlines. They were sometimes perforated at the base so that they could be slung on a thong at the artist's belt. Ground up paint could also be carried about in pots made from the tips of antelope horns, and one Bushman painter, who was killed during the struggle with the whites, had several of these pots dangling from his belt when he died. An analogy from Ethiopian illumination suggests how these pots could have been employed while painting was being done. The sharp end of the horn was thrust into the ground while the painter squatted beside it, just as an Ethiopian scribe did with his ink horn.

Other containers for dry powdered paint were earthenware pots, which have been already mentioned as containers of specular iron, ostrich egg shells, which were all-purpose containers for the Bushmen, and boxes made from small tortoiseshells, similar to those which the Bushmen of the Kalahari desert still make to sell to tourists.

The stone palettes used to grind up body paint were used to mix paint for making the pictures. These palettes are some of the many objects that remind us of the connection between rock painting and ancient Egypt.

It was probably the practice of painting themselves that had introduced the hunter artists to paint and the lasting quality of the binders employed. A barrier cream between the skin and the hot sun was an essential in Africa. Africans put pats of butter on their heads and they must have noticed that the resulting mixture of grease, and body paint, was very tenacious. Wood remarks of the Bushmen that "the sooty black hue that makes them appear nearly as dark as the Kaffirs" is made up from grease and the soot from their cooking fires.[1]

Bushwomen also clotted their hair with red ochre, mixed with grease, while Hottentots and Bushmen alike loved to plaster their very scanty hair with grease and paint, or clay, as a protection against the cold at night.

The tool with which the hunter artists applied their colors was either a bone palette knife or some kind of brush. I suggest elsewhere that the Hottentots, who must be included in the corps of rock painters, would not have to look far for a brush to use on the paintings because they employed one instead of a spoon to sup liquids. The Bushmen, too, were never without a brush in their hands, because they usually carried giraffe tails. Harris has described for us how the Bushman belle with whom he was so enamored used her giraffe tail as a handkerchief.

Other types of brushes were in use. In one of the few areas of Africa where any painting is still carried on, among the Wagogo of Tanzania, the modern painters use a stick whose end has been frayed into a brush, and the fat of a sacrificed beast to repaint the old signs on the cave walls. They explain that they carry out this custom, because the Wamia who preceded them used to do this. They do not know what the symbols mean but they believe that they are magic and will bring rain to them when they pray.[2]

The frayed-end brush is still used in other parts of Africa and many of the paintings on papyrus of the Ancient Egyptians, together with Ethiopian illuminations, were made with a reed that had been frayed at the end after being chewed.

Some observers have suggested that the rock painters must have used hair brushes as well because the lines of some of the paintings are so fine that they could have been made by no other means. A Bushman called Silayi did indeed tell a magistrate named W.E. Stanford in 1884 that the hairs taken

[1] Wood, *The Natural History of Man*, p. 267.
[2] Cole, *The Prehistory of East Africa*, pp. 226-27.

Several sets of painters, working at different times over a period of what may have been thousands of years, contributed to build up this frieze of paintings at the Menemba Cave in Rhodesia. The whole of the 150-foot wall of the cave is covered with human and animal figures. (Photo Courtesy Rhodesian Department of Information.)

from the tail or mane of a gnu were used tied together and fastened to a thin reed. The brush was then dipped in prepared clay and used to paint with. Ancient Egyptians did use hair brushes as well as the reed ones, at least toward the end of Egyptian history.

At least one other kind of brush was in use by the rock painters. "The tools of the Bushman," says J.G. Wood,[3] "are simple enough, consisting of a feather dipped in grease, in which he has mixed colored

clays." Most of the ostrich feathers worn in hats by ladies in America and England during Victorian times had indeed been obtained by the Bushmen, and because ostrich feathers were such an important item of trade the Bushmen had discovered a method of storing them, a method that may, of course, have been an extremely old one. The quill of an ostrich feather was inserted into a hollow reed. The end of the reed was tapped on the ground until the tip of the feather disappeared into it. An inch or two of feather, protruding from a holder of this sort, would make an ideal paintbrush, capable of painting the finest lines, yet having a handle that would never clog with paint.

It is much more difficult to reconstitute the painting methods used by the Bushmen than their palette and painting tools. Does a line drawn round the outline of an animal on the wall of a shelter indicate that this is the outline sketch that is to be

[3]Wood, *The Natural History of Man*, p. 298.

Some of the motifs of the cave paintings reappear, rather mysteriously, in Black African art. On this painted Bantu shield, "filiform men," similar to those used in cave paintings, can be discerned. (Photo Courtesy British Museum.)

Occasionally rock paintings reveal something of the technique by which they were made. In this painting at the Charewa Elephant Cave, in the Mtoko Area in Rhodesia, this group of elephants has been crudely drawn in outline with an infill of thick, off-white pigment. (Courtesy Rhodesian Department of Information.)

filled in in color, or was it merely the beginning of a monochrome silhouette? Why were some pictures silhouettes and others fully detailed? Why were some one color and others multicolored paintings?

We can be sure of one fact and that was that the artists painted directly onto the canvas. They did not use the preliminary drawings that have been found in prehistoric Europe in the form of pieces of bone or flat pebbles on which original ideas for paintings were noted first, then transferred to the cave walls. Where painted stones do exist, it is as burial stones and there are no paintings on the walls.

Sometimes, an undercoat of white was put on, then, the colors laid on top, but this was not invariably the case. There was no containing black outline to a picture, and, apparently, the colors were laid on side by side simultaneously. This would be a difficult technique for a modern painter, but it may have been a natural one for the artist to apply. He probably thought in color, and could, like the modern Eskimo, make a sketch of anything he had seen, such as a stretch of coastline. How else, indeed, could the hunter artists have drawn anything at all? They often painted in caves, in kloofs far out of sight of the game, or even in clefts in the rock so narrow that the painter had to lie on his back and paint in

such a cramped position that even if he had had a sketch with him, he could never have used it.

The technique of rock engraving is much more visible to the eye than that of painting. The term *engraving* is a little misleading, like many other terms of art, and observers have sought to substitute that of *petroglyph,* instead. Though the earliest engravings are just outline scratches, others are so boldly cut that they rank as sculpture rather than engraving and they inevitably recall the boldly cut monumental inscriptions and bas reliefs of ancient Egypt.

A rock engraving must have always been a work of considerable labor. Perhaps this is one reason that they are to be found more on the kopjes or hills of Africa rather than the caves. There are exceptions to this rule, as to most others in rock art, but it is at least possible to suggest that a kopje would be a much more central spot for a hunter than a cave. Game would be passing him in all directions, and, although he would have to break off his work in order to chase the animals he hunted, these interruptions need not be very long. Most of his food would be provided for him by his womenfolk anyway, as happens with the Kalahari Bushmen of today. He would hunt for three days of the week, but would be able to spend the rest of his time chipping away at his engraving.

This rhinoceros engraving is the product of a technique as meticulous and demanding as pointillisme. (Photo Courtesy British Museum.)

A pecked engraving of a giraffe from South Africa. (Photo Courtesy British Museum.)

It would be fascinating to know just why some artists chose the difficult way of engraving rather than the easier one of rock painting. One reason has been already suggested. The kopjes were not suitable for paintings because they did not contain caves. This marked distinction between the localities in which the two kinds of art are found led Stow to suppose (quite erroneously I feel) that there were two kinds of Bushmen, the cave Bushmen, who lived in rock shelters and created the cave paintings, and the kopje Bushmen who lived on top of the kopjes and made the engravings.

The very difficulty of the engraving must have been so great that it is tempting to assume that the artists chose this particular medium just because it was time consuming, as the old scrimshoners preferred to work with whales' teeth because a properly made whale's tooth would last the whole voyage home, keep the artist's mind happy and occupied, and give him something to show for it as a souvenir at the end, one which he could present to his wife or sweetheart.

Almost everything that one can surmise about the early rock painters seems to contradict the idea that they took to engraving because it was a time-consuming hobby. If one can judge, by comparison with the Bushmen, the early hunter artists had no great desire to work. They preferred to do the minimum necessary to keep themselves alive. As for pastime, there is every reason to suppose that the favored pastime of the Bushmen was not art, but music, dancing, and story telling. The reason the Bushmen did carry out their paintings was, I feel, not connected with a desire to pass the time. Their motives will be discussed at greater lengths later.

It is important to differentiate, at the outset, between pictorial or symbolic and functional engravings. Some engravings in Tanzania, Rhodesia, and elsewhere are held not to be proper engravings at all. They are grooves cut in the rock to make the task of grinding and polishing stone axes and adzes easier. These grooves are "V" or "U" shaped in section and they are cut in the rock cliffs where they occur in a fashion that suggests that the edge of a stone axe was pushed into them and then turned round and round in the groove to grind it into shape. Other cup-shaped hollows occur in rocks. These may be a form of abstract sculpture, suggested perhaps by the pot-holes that a river grinds in its bank by swirling round loose pebbles in small depressions until they become the size of saucepans or bathtubs, or, more likely they are holes specially shaped for pounding some comestible with a wooden pestle. The sound of wooden pestles beating wooden mortars is rarely absent from an African village, and it may be that there was a shortage of suitable wood for pestles in some areas so that stone was used instead. Other hollowed out depressions are said to be *mancala* boards. Mancala was an African game (which is still played) in which small pebbles or seeds are removed from one cup and placed in another. Engravings attributed to this purpose have been found in Zambia.

The least elaborate way of creating a rock engraving was to take a sharp, pointed stone and scratch a design on the cave wall. These engravings are supposed to be the earliest, and Holub, the Austrian savant who removed many engravings from South Africa, stated that triangular stone tools were used to cut the outline. Though straightforward, this method was still a laborious one in that the stone burin used to cut the line would need constant resharpening. Once cut, the design thus obtained was deepened by rubbing the tool in the groove until it had been incised to some considerable depth.

The rock artists were nothing if not painstaking and hard working. Whole galleries have been covered with engravings, as in this Zambian cave at Chifubwa. (Courtesy of Zambian Tourist Board.)

Other engravings were made by making a series of small holes, then joining them up with a continuous line. This technique so much resembles that of tattooing that once more it is interesting to speculate whether just as the paintings may have corresponded to body paintings, the engravings corresponded to tattoo patterns. The lines thus incised could be colored.

Another way of making an engraving was by just rubbing lines into a soft stone with a hard one, but the more usual kind of engraving took advantage of a geological peculiarity of South Africa. Many areas of the Republic contain hard rock, so hard that a diamond drill will only penetrate into the basic rock with the greatest difficulty. On hard rock such as this, however, rock like the diabase exposures at Driekops Eiland, weathering has occurred. The weathered surface was softer than that of the virgin rock. To cut their engravings on diabase, dolerite, or hornfels, the sculptors used tools of the same rock on which they

were engraving, tools that they picked up from the floor of the rock face, and worked up into a point by striking chips from them with other stones, resharpening them when they became blunt.

The characteristic engraving technique would combine silhouette with caricature, seizing all the essentials of the subject, usually an animal, in a bold outline. Detail would then be added by putting in a multitude of tiny dots, so as to outline the mane of an eland, for example, or adding internal lines to show up the shoulder blade of an animal.

Another technique made use of a combination of an intaglio, similar in feeling to that later employed by the Egyptian sculptors and a multitude of tiny dots, each made by a single peck applied with a pointed stone hammer.

In one of the most interesting techniques of all, cross hatching was added inside the outline. Surely this is exactly the same kind of engraving that is still carried out by the modern Kalahari Bushmen on their engraved ostrich eggs. Just such an egg, preserved in the National Museum in Bulawayo, Rhodesia, bears a scrimshawed design of a stylized crocodile. This connection between Bushmen and engraved rocks is important because, although Holub said the Bushmen were still making engravings, some observers have argued that those engravings which we have are far older than the time of the Bushmen.

Sometimes, the interior of an engraved outline would be polished. At other times, it would be painted. Both techniques also appear in ancient Egyptian sculpture.

Another engraving method, which is probably accidental, is to coat the surface of the rock with a sort of paint made up from bird droppings. As water percolates onto the engraved surface, the rock is eaten away by the acid in the bird lime and it remains rough in texture against the smooth rock.

A reason that so many of the engravings were apparently left blank, and not filled in with color, was that when first cut, an engraving stood out against the somber dolerite or deep red sandstone of the rock shelters with a white line, like a scraper board drawing today. Only gradually did the surface of the rock oxidize with time, so that the lines of the engraving took on a color indistinguishable from that of the background, the picture becoming a faint ghost, only visible in the slanting rays of the sun.

As the weathering process proceeds, not merely does the white line disappear from its dark background but the cuts themselves, once hard and "V" shaped, now become softened and rounded off. The action of wind-blown dust, the heats of summer and frosts of winter, complete the abrasion process. Parts of the design are lost — such as the tuft on the tail of a giraffe in one of my line drawings. The whole design, now less and less noticeable, can easily escape detection altogether, just as an engraving of double axes at Stonehenge escaped countless generations of visitors to that best known of British ancient monuments and was only discovered in our own day. This may be one reason that there are many fewer engravings known than paintings — they have simply escaped detection. One suspects, moreover, that the engraving, unprotected by an overhang, like the painting in its rock shelter, is so much more vulnerable that many more have been lost through exfoliation.

Moreover, not every rock surface was considered suitable to engrave by the artists. In Rhodesia, for example, granite, on which the painters loved to paint, was avoided by the engravers. Instead, hard sandstones, quartz, greywacke, and talc schists were sought out. Because these stones were not available everywhere, there are no engravings where they are absent.

4

The Subjects of Rock Art

So many animals appear in the rock galleries of Africa that it is easy to see why George William Stow believed that the paintings were a record of the totems of the Bushman. It may well be that there are more animals than we can recognize. Some of the schematized paintings can be recognized to be of animals through some element of caricature, such as the long neck of a giraffe. Other paintings, apparently so abstract as to be quite unrecognizable, may bear an animal origin. I have already referred to the mysterious pictures at Mwalawolemba, which may represent animals within a *kraal.*

The fact that the hunter artists spent at least three days a week in pursuit of game contributed to this choice of subject. So, too, did the fondness the Bushmen felt for animals. The painters were able to integrate their paintings with their subjects in an astonishing fashion by painting the animals with their own vital juices, while they also felt much more relaxed when painting animals, since when painting humans, their hands were tied by the taboos regarding human portraiture.

The artists have rendered an invaluable service by portraying extinct animals such as the *Bubalus antiqus,* the quagga and the deer. There may be more extinct animals that appear in the Tassili paintings but we cannot recognize them as such. It seems quite possible, for example, that the hippopotamus repre-sented at Tassili is a distinct subspecies. The big pachyderms might have escaped southwards from the dessication of their territory, but it is difficult to imagine a hippopotamus crossing the dried-up Sahara.

Tassili paintings, early and later, are also invaluable in that they depict existing species thousands of years ago. The animals shown, giraffe, dogs, moufflons, and so forth, seem to have changed very little. Antelopes, oryx, and gazelle can easily be recognized. There are also Hamitic greyhounds, a full-breasted, pointy-eared, slim-legged dog that appears not merely at Tassili but also in the art of Ancient Egypt during the fourth to sixth dynasties.

The longhorn cattle, which formed the staff of life to the Tassilians, almost deserve to rank as an extinct species, because they seem to have left no direct descendants, even though they may have been assimi-lated into the Zebu cattle strain.

Other than at Tassili, extinct animals are to be found in African rock art. In the Sahara, at Tibesti, a rock engraving shows an extinct elk, *Megaceroides algericus.* Paintings of stags at the Cave of the Wild Boar and in other parts of Ethiopia bear witness to the temporary survival of a Mediterranean species of deer that wandered south before extinction. The quagga, which is easily confused with the zebra, may appear farther south.

It is indeed only in South and Central Africa that

the full riches of animal painting can be seen. Rock shelters in these regions are a game park in fresco, and as in a real game park it is not always possible to see all the animals, or not all at one time. Nor is it always possible to be quite sure of identification, because as has been noticed, the painter was quick to throw the veil of unreality between his subject and the spectator.

As in a game park, too, some animals never appear to be seen even though a list of the fauna in the region mentions them. Just as the game warden always has a story ready to explain why the absentees are not there ("All the elephants have gone to Mozambique,)" so observers have pointed to those fauna missing from the cave walls and speculated as to why they should be absent.

Something has already been said about the hyrax, which was an important animal in Bushman mythology, yet which only appears once or twice. Not merely was it important from the point of view of folklore, it was also, apparently, the most important item in the food of the early hunters. Innumerable bones and skulls of the beast occur in the middens of the cave folk.

The same could be said of the tortoise, which was the single most common item of diet for the rock artists. Yet Cooke has estimated that it was only represented twice on a rock wall.[1] Could it have been, as I have suggested elsewhere, that the hyrax was too sacred to be painted? Was it because its solidified urine was an important element in arrow poison and it would have been unwise to picture it on a rock wall for fear of giving enemies a clue to the jealously guarded formula? Did the cave artists fear to represent the hyrax and the tortoise, just because they spread their karosses on floors thickly littered with their bones, and to paint them might awake revengeful ghosts?

Nobody could claim that the nature paintings on the rock shelters are representative of African nature as a whole. Where, for example, are the insects, so conspicuous by their presence in the real Africa, so notable by their absence in the pictured one? There is a spider in Tassili, there are flying insects in Rhodesia, but once more, if sympathetic magic were the motive of the paintings then one would expect to find a lot more insects, as one would rock rabbits, because the hunter artists lived largely upon them. It is true that there are some edible insects such as locusts and termites, which appear in the pictures.

Other animals that suffer neglect from the painters, though they played a large part in their life and diet, were cane rats, ant bears, and spring hares, even though pictures of men carrying the flexible hooked sticks used to dislodge these hares from their burrows do occur in southwest Africa and Rhodesia.[2]

In the bird kingdom, too, there are many significant omissions. Small birds must have played just as large a part in the diet of the painters as they do in Africa today, where every child sets his snare for them, and eats them raw if he is lucky enough to catch one. Game birds such as the francolin and the guinea fowl are also absent. What the artists seem to have been interested in was large birds, such as the ostrich, which occurs again and again, the European stork, and the whale headed stork, which occurs in at least two instances.

Where the artists really did feel at home was in their portrayal of big game. These form the stock in trade of all cave painters, but their principles of selection are at first difficult to disentangle. If it is true that large carnivores hardly ever appear (only ten have been recorded for the whole of the Drakensberg), a fact that encourages the sympathetic magic school, who feel that they were not portrayed because the painters were afraid of bringing them to life, other dangerous animals appear, such as the buffalo, the most savage animal of the African jungle, the python, and the crocodile. If the painters were afraid of portraying an animal for fear that they might give it life, just as sailors did not whistle lest they conjure up a wind, why were these noxious animals included? The second most favorite animal was the eland.[3] Next comes the horse (in the Drakensberg) and other big antelopes. In a way, the elephant was the biggest favorite, because it is distributed all over Africa. Kudu, roan antelope, and sable antelope are worth mentioning by name. The zebra is often depicted, as is the giraffe. The white rhinoceros, black rhinoceros, and hippopotamus are widely distributed. Animals of minor importance include the oribi, hartebeest, tsassebe, impala, and wildebeest, some of which have been noticed under the category of small antelopes.

[2]Ibid., p. 34

[1]C.K. Cooke, *Rock Art of Southern Africa* (Cape Town: Books of Africa, 1969), p. 33.

[3]I have followed the schedule given by the Rudners, p. 267, showing "Distribution of Animal Pictures" in *The Rock Art of Southern Africa.*

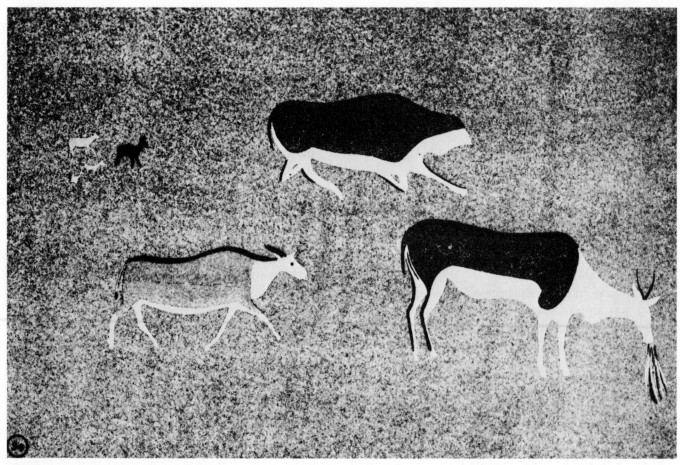

Eland and bucks, one of which may be a "rain animal." (Painting by Helen Tongue. Photo by Stella Mayes Reed.)

Fish of various species appear, of which the most striking depictions are those of whales and dolphins from the Southern Cape.

Great numbers of domesticated animals appear in South Africa. The horse has been already mentioned. There are also long-tailed sheep and humped cattle, belonging to the Hottentots, Bantu cattle, and the mules and oxen of the white trekkers.

Altogether, the reason that some animals were selected and others passed over for painting is difficult to establish. Some animals that must have been seen very frequently, such as the night apes, were never portrayed. Others that were very important for food, such as caterpillars, still dried and exported to mineworkers in South Africa as a rare delicacy, have been left out, as, apparently, have been ostrich eggs.

The number of elands represented upholds the contention I put forward in the chapter on "The Purpose of the Paintings," that the paintings were essentially religious in origin. They attempted to portray the Bushman god Kaggen, by indicating his presence through the herds of eland. What the artists were out to depict was the life force of the animals they represented, as well as that of trees, rocks, and even objects such as possessions, all of which were "alive" to a primitive. Since it was the life force that was being portrayed, the color of the subject was unimportant, an animal could be painted in any color, and usually was. So, too, was the scale of the painting, this need not be realistic, though some animals were painted very large indeed.

What about the choice of animal? It seems that, to some extent, number and size governed this choice. Elands always ran in herds, so besides their association with the god Kaggen, elands would have a multiplicity of life force. A large elephant might be considered as possessing greater life force than a small insect. It was certainly harder to kill. This principle held good for fish and birds as well. The pencil of the Bushman labored more lovingly on the contours of

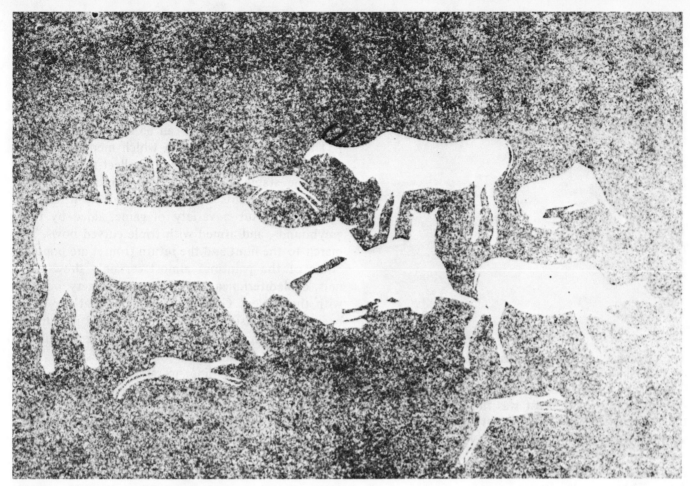

Elands, rhebucks, and oxen, part of a continuous picture from Catherine's Post. (Painting by Helen Tongue. Photo by Stella Mayes Reed.)

Elephant, bontebuck, and hartebeest. Baviaan's Krantz. (Painting by Helen Tongue. Photo by Stella Mayes Reed.)

The elephant occurs in rock paintings from every part of Africa — as in this South African cave painting. One reason for its popularity as a subject may have been that this great beast was full of the life force that cave artists may have sought to portray. (Photo Courtesy South African Tourist Board.)

that great animal, the whale, than it did on shellfish (which were never represented) even though whole tribes of Bushmen depended on shellfish for their diet.

So much for the main principle behind the choice of subject. The interpretation of particular subjects is notoriously difficult in that it is subjective. The meaning placed on a picture — even a black and white photograph — by an individual will vary very much with his outlook in life. In an outmoded test in psychology, called the "thematic appreciation test," students were shown a photograph of police clashing with strikers. The more conservative-minded ones said that law and order had to be maintained somehow and that regrettably, violence sometimes had to be used to do this. More radically inclined students wrote essays on "police brutality" shown to the "innocent workers."

In the same way, a rock painting is all things to all men, and its interpretation is almost always controversial. At Tassili, for example, Brennan's reading of a particular scene was that a girl was being sold into prostitution. She was hanging back reluctantly, while her vendor took the basket of cowries that was the price of the sale in such a way as to reveal a sense of shame. A later interpreter of Tassili has not hesitated to qualify this description of what is happening in the picture as "fantastic."

In spite of this suggestion of mine that caution

may be necessary in interpreting most of the rock paintings, there are some that are apparently so straightforward that they can be readily understood.

There are many scenes in which men or women, armed with digging sticks, go to collect the roots that were the staple diet of the old hunters. The most sophisticated hunts occur in the north, where the Tassilians pursue a variety of game, aided by their greyhounds, and armed with triple curved bows. The march to the hunt and the return from it are popular. Some of the paintings almost certainly show game nets, a Mediterranean hunting method very popular with the ancient Greeks and Romans that may have been used in Asia as well. I have looked in vain for any picture that I could be sure represents hunters armed with feathered brooms, devices that were placed in a long line to scare game toward a prearranged spot where they would fall over a precipice or be shot by hidden archers. Some hunters imitate the action of baboons to approach their quarry, others dress in ostrich skins and perhaps in

Hottentot mother leaning on a digging stick (usually weighted by a stone). Many sticks of this sort appear in paintings. From Wood. (Photo by Stella Mayes Reed.)

Men and women with digging sticks, and a leopard bleeding at the mouth, which may be a "rain animal." (Painting by Helen Tongue. Photo by Stella Mayes Reed.)

buck heads and hides as well, so as to camouflage their stealthy approach to their prey through long elephant grass. Some figures have their hair stuck through with arrows, in the manner of the historic Bushmen, others carry throwing sticks (at Tassili) or long sticks with hooks for hauling hares from their burrows. While some hunters are apparently engaged in stampeding game, which afterwards appears trapped between two boulders as though it had fallen from a cliff, others cut up the spoils of the hunt. Hunters wear, on their heads, masks made from the heads of the animals they have killed.

Other paintings deal with fishing, and show fish spears and fish traps.

Not all the people on the shelter walls are hunters. Some are probably dancing, possibly in masks. Some are sitting in the shade, which, like dancing, is still a popular pastime in Africa. Some are trekking, either engaged in seasonal migration, say between the shore to eat shellfish and the kopjes to catch game, or bound on longer journeys. There is no way of knowing just how long the journey is going to be because the Bushmen liked to travel light and carry only essentials such as a skin bag (figured in the paintings), weapons (which also appear), and knobkerries, which one observer states were only used by the Bushmen for beating their wives.

Man dragging thongs or skins and an elephant upside down. Baviaan's Krantz. (Painting by Helen Tongue. Photo by Stella Mayes Reed.)

In this pecked engraving of an ostrich hunt from South Africa, the long stick held by the human figure may represent one of the wands tipped with ostrich feathers, used to scare animals during game drives. (Photo Courtesy South African Tourist Board.)

Lots of people appear who may be engaged in conferences. Other figures sit with a regal attitude, apparently carrying insignia and receiving the homage of subjects.

There are plenty of scenes of battles, though, as in so much rock art, it is a little difficult to see what is actually happening and some have suggested that scenes of battle or dueling at Tassili may be simply ritual dances, such as those carried on by armed dancers called the "Salii" in ancient Rome. Some commentators have tried to divide the peaceful and warlike scenes into particular sequences.

Most difficult of all to interpret are those scenes which may partake of magic, mythology, ceremonial, or initiation. Even the many cattle scenes of Tassili may reflect sacrifice rather than stock rearing. The cattle and sheep that appear in so many later paintings may have been sacrifices, too, and the very

The white dots surrounding this buffalo may represent a trap. (Photo Courtesy Ministry of National Education, Tanzania.)

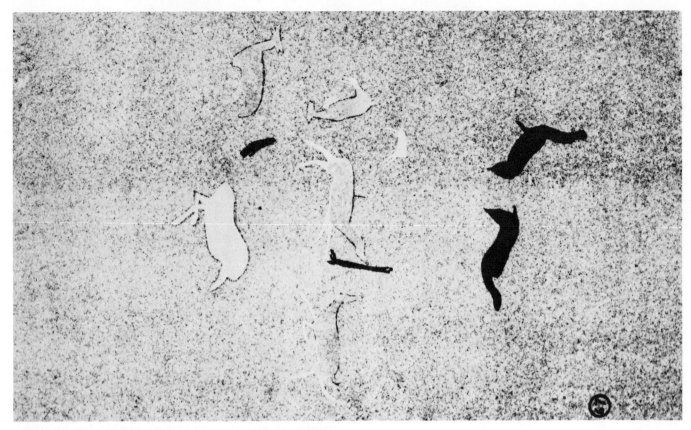

Bucks falling into a pit used for trapping game.
(Painting by Helen Tongue. Photo by Stella Mayes
Reed.)

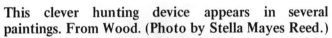

This clever hunting device appears in several
paintings. From Wood. (Photo by Stella Mayes Reed.)

Sometimes, the subject of rock painting is the techniques used by hunters. Here, an early hunter painter, disguised as an ostrich, approaches his prey—but there is something about his intruder that has alarmed the flock, and all the birds have turned to look closely at the stranger. From a painting by Stow. (Courtesy British Museum.)

unpopular Bushmen habit of killing all the cattle that they could not steal may have been due to a desire to sacrifice them to their god. That is, at least, as likely an explanation as any so far put forward.

I have argued already that in a sense all painting was religious. It was intended not merely to mark the presence of the god Kaggen, but also to proclaim and delimit the sacred area, like a spire and a churchyard today.

"The artists," writes Yolande Tschudi, of Tassili, "only executed their works on certain areas of the surface of the rocks areas that we may call 'conse-crated.' It is because of this that, as one has found them in the prehistoric art of Europe, so too at Tassili, one finds the paintings one beside another or even one on top of another. They only cover part of the rock surfaces, of which many, though possessing an aspect and a quality very favorable for being embellished, have, nonetheless, remained untouched."

It is one thing to suggest that all rock paintings are

A Bushman wearing poisoned arrows in his hair. (Photo by Stella Mayes Reed.)

It is tempting to see in the strange form to the left of the reclining man a fish trap like the ones still used in Lake Malawi. From a cave in the Mtoko Area of Rhodesia. (Photo Courtesy Rhodesian Ministry of Information.)

A procession of dancing or marching figures, though stylized, depict steatopygia. (Painting by Helen Tongue. Photo by Stella Mayes Reed.)

62

This scene of human figures with an animal from Tanzania may represent an "abduction," as has been surmised, or perhaps some ceremonial ritual. (Photo Courtesy Ministry of Education, Tanzania.)

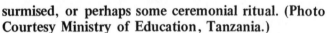

religious in origin, and quite another to select from them scenes that might be thought to concern themselves with ceremonial or magic.

Those at Tassili are so representational that they lend themselves much more to interpretation than pictures farther south. Commentators have seen in them representations of the moon waxing and waning, of cows representative of the Cow Goddess, worshipped in prehistoric Egypt, of the cockerel, also an object of divinity, of women painted in an unnatural pose that could symbolize either conception or maternity, some of whom have been rendered steatopygous as a fertility wish. The scenes of couples making love are also, it would seem, connected with fertility, while even such an apparently everyday object as a jar of milk could have its religious

This picture from the Battle Cave may illustrate a real defense of the actual cave in which it is painted. Attackers without women are met by defenders with women—some of whom try to hold two of the men back perhaps because they are too young. (Photo Courtesy South African Tourist Agency.)

Arrows fly through the air in this scene from the
Battle Cave, Drakensberg. (Photo Courtesy South
African Tourist Agency.)

Subjects such as this one, from South Africa, usually described as "sorcerers" or "witch doctors," play a mysterious part in cave art. They are all the more mysterious because of the fact that the Bushmen did not possess witch doctors. (Photo Courtesy South African Tourist Board.)

significance, because of the part that milk played in contemporary religious cults, and also, it may be added, in the religion of the Hottentots.

It is much more difficult to pick out magical scenes away from the Sahara. While it has been suggested, for example, that figures with hair hanging down over their faces who accompany hunters may be medicine men come out to secure good fortune in the hunt, the Bushmen did not have medicine men or witch doctors — though, of course, the hunter painters who preceded them may have.

Like magic, mythology is a sort of Tom Tiddler's Ground for interpretations of pictures. Almost any picture can be wrenched into a mythological context. Alexander R. Willcox, the most eloquent of mythological interpreters, has argued that several of the amorphous-looking beasts that appear in the paintings

are rain animals.[4] Since he himself has explained, however, the legs of a rain animal are columns of descending rain, and the only part of any picture that he can point to as rain takes the form of lines issuing from the *mouth* of an animal, I cannot feel that this identification will hold fast.

Even Stow, who tried to explain most aspects of the shelter paintings, could make nothing of the dots and dashes in the schematic paintings, which he called "the greatest mystery of rock art." Nor could he make much of the abstract forms.

These have been referred to more than once. While some look like a maze, others are shaped like ladders. Some, usually finger paintings, take the form of rows of dots or dashes in pairs, or in larger numbers, and they are sometimes arranged in single lines. Many

This mythological figure in a pecked engraving may be that of a "tokolosh," a nightmare creature from contemporary folklore. Many of the mythological ideas of the original engravers and painters may have passed into modern times. From Vryburg, South Africa. (Photo Courtesy South African Tourist Board.)

[4]Willcox, *South Africa*, p. 33.

88

A strange sorcerer figure from Diana's Vow Cave near Rusape, Rhodesia. (Photo Courtesy Rhodesian Ministry of Information.)

A snake—probably a mythical one — and women with digging sticks. (Painting by Helen Tongue. Photo by Stella Mayes Reed.)

Lively game animals combine with the dots that Stow called the "real mystery" of rock art in this painting from Maydale Farm, Robert Macilwaine National Park near Salisbury, Rhodesia. (Courtesy Rhodesian Ministry of Information.)

Sorcerers and the "nose bleeding" after the nose bleeding dance. See the discussion of Klingender's interpretation of this picture. (Painting by Helen Tongue. Photograph by Stella Mayes Reed.)

These strange dots were probably executed by finger painting. To touch them is to put oneself directly in contact with the artist who painted them, perhaps a millenia ago. (Photo Courtesy Zambia National Tourist Board.)

These strange symbols are among the most compelling problems set by any art. (Courtesy of Malawi Tourist Board.)

observers felt that the dashes stood for liquid. Willcox felt they represented rain. Klingender thought they were dropping blood. Others have found yet another meaning in them, water or rivers.

Since the dashes represent nothing recognizable, I would hazard a guess that they stood for a concept that could not be rendered representationally — the spirit of life itself. They often issue from creatures' mouths, so the hunter painters may have equated "breath" with "life." As for the dots, I have a theory that would account for them, too. My view is that rock painting is one of the contact arts. Just as one would be expected to kiss the painted face of an icon in order to receive a blessing from it, so I feel he or she would also be expected to touch the painted or engraved footprints and handprints, or the finger painted dots and dashes, which are such a feature of rock art. By so doing, one would be put into direct contact with the men of old (now deified ancestors) who had made these works of art and become charged with the vital spirit that had inspired them.

What about the more elaborate schematic designs, which have been variously christened "geometric," "tectiform" formlings, "or cryptomorphs?" They have been compared to grain bins, kraals, shield patterns, rock shelters, quivers, and many other objects. Some of them look so like maps or diagrams that it is tempting to assume that this was what they were. The ancient hunters, however, were probably able to carry their maps in the head, and if they were not they would hardly be likely to paint them up on the wall of a shelter for everyone to see. It would be equally tempting to regard these diagrams as star maps, and some have felt that they represented sun symbols.

Animals became more and more stylized as time progressed. What began as a realistic animal ended up looking more like a letter of the alphabet or a Roman numeral. Symbols may have gone through the same process of being simplified until any resemblance to the original form was lost. During the times of trouble and disturbance, when peoples to whom the painters belonged were being supplanted by stronger invaders, the painters may have decided to represent symbolically what it was no longer safe to paint in a realistic way.

5

An Imaginary Tour of the Rock Galleries

An imaginary journey around the galleries of rock art scattered throughout Africa will, I hope, introduce my readers to the incredible riches of the continent, and also enable them to find some unity in the diversity that they display.

Much more will be said, in this journey, about paintings than about engravings. The paintings are much more numerous, they treat a wider range of subjects, and they are much more detailed and much more expanded in their view of any subject than the engravings, which are usually of but a single figure. In a word, paintings have much more to teach the observer than do engravings.

Are the rock galleries scattered haphazardly throughout Africa? By no means. Their location follows a particular pattern or plan that has often been observed in the past by commentators. The area of Africa covered by rock painting sites is a great crescent-shaped belt that runs from the West coast, from a point equivalent to Cape Verd, across the Sahara, passing south of Lake Chad, then turns south and passes between the Great Lakes and the Indian Ocean till it reaches the Zambezi. Then the area of rock painting turns westward and runs till it reaches the Atlantic coast near Benguela. Between the Niger and the Zambezi, there is a vast area in which hardly any paintings are to be found. As has often been

observed in the past, this area is coterminous with the range of the tsetse fly. This insect, a blood-sucking fly, preys on humans and animals alike, and it carries sleeping sickness and the tsetse fly disease. More than one African conqueror has been turned back by the tsetse. Mzilikazi, the Matabele war lord who invaded Makololand in the early nineteenth century, was turned back not so much by the resistance of the Malolo as by the decimation of his herds by the tsetse flies.

The inference to be drawn from the overlapping of the tsetse and rock painting areas on the map of Africa is that the rock painters were dependent either on cattle or big game (which the tsetse attacks) but especially the latter. The migration of herdsmen from the Sahara region and the Horn of Africa southward, accompanied by their flocks and herds, might, it is thought, have contributed to the spread of rock painting.

There are several drawbacks to this theory, however. First, the area of the tsetse and the rock painter do not correspond exactly. There are rich areas of painting well inside the fly-infested belt, especially on the east coast. Furthermore, the tsetse map has been drawn with the *present* distribution of the insect in mind. We really have no evidence that it did not once have a much wider homeland. It may have existed in the Sahara, and disappeared from that region with the southward movement of the game caused by dessication of the now desert area in the same way that it is supposed to have disappeared from other parts of Africa because of the killing off of most of the game by white hunters. What is more, there is little to connect the last of the rock painters, the Bushmen, with flocks and herds. They liked to eat beef, but it was the beef of other peoples' cows. On the other hand, the Hottentots, their near relatives and fellow painters, were herdsmen.

It is much more difficult to discover a rock painting in the dense forests of equatorial African than on the naked sides of a kopje out on the open veldt. This may be one reason that so few painted sites have been found in West Africa and also so few rock engraving sites.

There may be other reasons. I feel that it is no accident that the West, the timber carrying region, is devoid of rock paintings because I feel that in that area the place of the rock shrine is taken by the timber temple. There is no need to decorate the walls of caves because everyone lives in houses, unlike the Bushmen or the Hottentots. The meeting place between rupestral (rock) art and parietal (house wall) art is in South Africa. Here the Basutos and other Africans plastered the walls of their houses and painted pictures on them. Left to himself, a Bantu worker in a Rhodesian mine will do the same thing. I give as illustrations some of these wall pictures, which, it will be seen, are not very different from the silhouette animals that occur in so many of the cave paintings. There was, then, according to my view at least, no need for there to be any rock paintings in the forest areas of Africa at all — rock painting and house painting were complementary to one another.

In spite of this general rule, there are exceptions. In the cave of Mbafu in the lower Congo, where the Ba Kongo tribe lives, paintings have been found embodying Christian symbols such as crosses, the crucifix, the XP motif, and even a standing figure that has been identified, plausibly, as that of Don Henrique, the first Congolese bishop, consecrated in 1518.

Another area that is an exception is Angola. Here at Pungo Adonga in Angola, in the middle of the mopane forest, near to the Cuanza River, are the Black Rocks, a natural acropolis formed of great red sandstone rocks, some of them 270 feet or more high. This fortress corresponds to that other natural fortress the "Acropolis" of Zimbabwe. This was the stronghold of the Jinga tribe, who held out for so long against Portuguese domination under their famous Queen, Anna Xinga, who ruled Angola between 1624 to 1633. It is many years since I defended the Queen in print from the charge hurled at her by her enemies, the charge of cannibalism. I was able to prove, to my own satisfaction at least, that she was not a cannibal but a ceremonial blood drinker — something very different. Anna Xinga has, since that time, become much more famous in America because she has been credited with the invention, or at least popularization of the well-known "Afro" hair style. At Pungo Andongo, however, she is principally remembered for some engraved footprints in the rock. These footprints, engraved on a rock floor between two giant boulders, are much too old to have any connection with Anna Xinga, but the idea of a footprint, associated with some great person of the past, is an interesting one to which I will return later. Meanwhile, it is sufficient to notice that, in spite of possessing such wonderful engravings, Angola also has what is probably the best school of parietal painting in Africa, indicating that the two kinds of art can overlap.

There is one obvious factor that determines the existence of rock paintings and engravings, the existence of suitable rock for both. Even though, as will be seen, only a tiny fraction of the suitable surfaces in an area are taken up by rock art, regions that are complete grassland, or desert, will have no paintings or engravings at all.

Rock art in Africa starts at the very northwest, in the Canary Islands, runs along Algeria and Tunisia, is found in great abundance in mountainous regions such as the Atlas, Tassili, Fezzan, Tibesti, and Uweinat, continues down the Nile (where paintings of gazelles domesticated by Neolithic folk are to be found side by side with the pious inscriptions of Coptic anchorites), extends into East Africa from Tanzania, Uganda, and Kenya to Ethiopia and the Horn of Africa, then ventures south into Zambia, Malawi, and Rhodesia, culminating, as many may feel in the paintings of South Africa, paintings that are to be found in such classic sites as the Brandberg, the Drakensberg, and the South West.

It will not be possible to visit all the rock sites of Africa, even in an imaginary excursion such as this. In the group I have selected, I have tried to hold the balance between famous localities such as Tassili, which everyone who goes to Africa will want to see for himself, and a few of the lesser known ones.

THE GRAND KABYLIE

Among the most remote galleries of rock art is the notable corpus of rock paintings and engravings to be found in the *Grande Kabylie* or Greater Kabylia, in northwest Africa. This region, which covers an area of seven thousand square miles, lies between Algiers, the capital of Algéria, and the Tunisian border.

Its thousands of paintings and engravings were discovered due to the repeated expeditions of R. Poyto and J.C. Musso, who in 1965-67 discovered painted sites in particularly difficult areas where it is possible to get to the painted rock shelters and *oued* walls only by scaling their perpendicular surfaces.

The Rudners have remarked very pertinently that the best rock art is to be found in "places of refuge and sanctuaries"[1] and the Grand Kabylie is a case in point. In this mountainous region, the underlying beds of gniess and micaschists are covered with a layer of Numidian sandstone. The peaks include the highest mountain in Algeria, except for one in the Hoggar, and the lower slopes of the hills are covered with forests of oak.

At the present moment, the tortured pinnacles of the crags in which the shelter and cave paintings are to be found seem to be about as inhospitable a spot as any on earth. In the era of the hunter artists, however, they did not lack two amenities that were much appreciated, abundant fresh water (the Oued Sebaon, which flows through the region, is one of the largest rivers in Algeria), and plenty of game.

Grand Kabylia has always been an area cut off from the rest of Algeria, as a glance at its structure will show, and it has usually been able to maintain its independence. It is noteworthy, for example, that when all the rest of North Africa was not merely Christian, but fervidly so, that Kabylia remained pagan.

When they explored the region, Poyto and Musso were struck by the fact that the painters had avoided painting in those rock shelters which were formed in crystalline or chalky rocks, though the shelters concerned were in well-wooded areas with an abundance of water. The rock surfaces also seemed to offer a good canvas for pictures, but in this kind of geological structure the painters had ignored them, though they had in a very few instances been prepared to make use of volcanic rock such as basalt.

With these few exceptions, the painters had chosen to work exclusively on surfaces of Numidian sandstone. Though Poyto and Musso do not draw any conclusions from their observations, it seems very probable that the permanency of the paintings was very important to the artists. They were looking, as I hope to indicate, for sites that were important by reason of their sanctity, but, just as you cannot build a church in a quagmire, it was essential that they should have the right background for the pictures.

The archaeologists also pointed out that not all the shelters that could have received ornamentation had in fact done so. Perfectly habitable caves, of the right geological setting, with easy access, and offering splendid painting surfaces had been passed by, and others, tiny, badly-lit crevices in the rock that could only be gained by footholds hacked in the stone, had received paintings.

The discoverers of the paintings pointed out that this enigma could be solved by the assumption that some of the painted shelters represented sacred sites. In support of this contention, they put forward the fact that the rock shelters corresponded both to sites of the local stone age industry and to country sanctuaries that were still venerated by the local people. Every painted site was associated with a locality that contained an abundance of oak mast (wind fallen acorns) on which early game must have fed. What was more striking still, the characters that were painted in the rock shelters, or some of them, were still used in local magic. The cross, for example, which had no connection with Christianity, figured largely.[2]

As for the almost inaccessible rock shelters reached by hand and footholds chiseled in the cliff face, Poyto and Musso had an interesting theory to account for them. They remarked on the fact that the floor of these caves had often been chiseled away to provide a flatter surface, and suggested that these tiny niches in the rock were, in fact, burial cases where a body had been left to be reduced to a skeleton before being buried elsewhere.

The Grand Kabylie is not the only region where painted caves are associated with shrines of some local cult. Rainmaking ceremonies are associated with some of the painted shelters in Rhodesia at the

---

[1] J. and I. Rudner, *The Hunter and His Art*, p.3.

[2] R. Poyto et J. C. Musso, *Memoires Du Centre De Recherches Athropologiques, Prehistoriques Et Ethnographiques*. Conseil De La Recherche Scientifique En Algérie, Vol. XII Corpus Des Peintures Et Gravuers Rupestres De Grande Kabylie (Paris: Arts Et Metiers Graphiques, 1969), p. 109.

Matopos, while paintings in the Soutpansberg in South Africa are visited by barren women who hang up bracelets as offerings. The women have no idea what the paintings mean and this is the case for Africa as a whole. In Malawi, for example, local people point to the rock pictures and say, "These paintings were made by the Bakatwa or Batwa, four-hundred to five-hundred years ago. These people were living here until a hundred and fifty years ago, and then they were all destroyed by the chief of the Chewa called Mkanda."

Such a tradition may either be correct or just a convenient story to account for the paintings. Most Bantu Africans are, today, completely apathetic about the rock paintings and feel quite disassociated from them — possibly because they feel guilt on account of the extermination of the painters (probably Bushman or Bushmanoid people) by their ancestors.

Just a few have kept up their religious associations with the cave paintings. Such scattered evidence that we possess, then, suggests that, instead of the cave paintings having been made for the purposes of sympathetic magic, the African paintings may serve to mark a shrine or confer a blessing.

The pictures or symbols, painted or engraved on the rock, could be considered of permanent amuletic value, signs that could confer good luck to anyone beholding them. Cave paintings have been considered to fulfill just this religious role elsewhere. At the Caves of the Thousand Bhuddas in China, for example, camel drivers from desert caravans used to enter the caves, stare at the paintings, then touch one of the statues for luck.

An interesting corollary of the view that the paintings and symbols that presumably resuméd all that the paintings had to say were amuletic would be the placing of a painted cave in good hunting country. The area where the Kabylie caves are situated was once rich in game and pasture for cattle because oak mast abounds there. A cave filled with symbols would become a permanent "magic light-house," attracting animals from a distance toward the hunter. A modern equivalent of such a cave, on the plane of reality, would be water piped to a pool in a game park that attracts animals to a place where visitors can watch them from a hide.

If amuletic signs were placed high up, then they could be seen from a greater distance and their influence would be correspondingly greater. Many of the cave paintings and symbols have been set quite high up. They are either in a cave, placed halfway up the side of a mountain, or they are painted well up on the wall of the cave, sometimes fifteen feet above the floor, suggesting that a ladder had to be used to paint them.

Archaeologists have always been puzzled as to why anyone should take so much trouble to paint a picture far above the ground. They have also been puzzled by overpaintings or "superpositions." Why should anyone want to spoil a good painting by placing it on top of another that would distract the observer's attention? While some observers have suggested that good painting surfaces were in very short supply, we have just seen that there was no shortage of good painting rock faces at Kabylie, but many of them went unpainted.

However, if the overpainting was similar in nature to the repainting that goes on in some East African caves all would then become clear. It could then be seen as a magical renewal of the charms of the cave, a

Paintings are often well above floor level, as in this example from Matopos, Rhodesia, at the Iswatugi cave. (Photo Courtesy Rhodesian Ministry of Information.)

96

spiritual strengthening of what had been done before, like the rededication of a church. When we come to Tassili, it will be seen that some of the painted figures on the walls of the caves are deities, or are assumed to be so.

What about the suggestion that some caves, at least, were charnel houses, chapels of ease, in which a body rested until decomposition, and scavenging hyenas and birds had disposed of it? It would certainly be a practice not without parallel in many other societies, such as among the Parsees, for example, who expose their dead on "Towers of Silence," and who have certainly visited Africa in times past.

Though modest by comparison with some of the richer sites like Tassili, the Grand Kabylie paintings are a very good introduction to rock art as a whole because they display the kinds of paintings that are to be found all over Africa. Some of the rocks show red ochre silhouettes of men, stylized to the point of being almost unrecognizable, without shading or polychrome work inside the basic outline. Some figures exhibit enormous *phalli*. The sexual aspects of rock painting are never entirely absent in any part of Africa. Though the Rudners have claimed that pictures of mating and sexual symbols are very rare in South Africa, this may be due to the prurient iconoclasm of Calvinist settlers and bowdlerizing clerics — like the Victorian canons of Chester cathedral who at the time South Africa was being opened up, burned some of the wood carvings in the cathedral because they considered them obscene. It is worth reminding ourselves that many of the prayers addressed to all deities have to do with sex or fertility. Hence, there need be nothing surprising in finding pictures of couples mating in caves in the Tassili, which I shall try to suggest were in fact shrines.

Animal silhouettes are also well represented at Kabylie, but they are so conventionalized that only a few can be recognized for what they are, cattle or jackals. Prominent among the paintings are some that I shall describe as "dots and dashes." These schematized designs appear all over Africa. The dots, which are apparently imprinted by the finger point, are arranged in single or multiple lines or grouped into ovals or circles. The dashes are also ranged in horizontal or vertical lines. Crosses are frequently painted, so is the outline of a hand, and it is worthwhile noticing that the palm print, known as the "hand of Fatima," is still widely used as a good

luck charm in North Africa. Arrows are a popular motif, and so are ovals. Then there are the strange symbols called "formlings," or more descriptively, "Frobenius' cigars" (after the German ethnographer who did so much work in Africa in the thirties). These strange symbols are to be found all over Africa and no one has ever produced a satisfactory explanation of what they represent. I feel they could be leaf shapes, because I consider that there might be quite a simple explanation for many of the problems of rock art. I recollect that once, when climbing a mountain in Africa, I picked up a dry leaf that had been attacked by mildew. The pattern of concentric circles that was thus formed was identical to one of the designs I had just been looking at in a cave painting. Besides these concentric circles, comb-shaped, square, or indefinite forms are to be found at Grand Kabylie.

As in other North African rock sites, Libyco-Berber characters form the last stage in the evolutions of the paintings. What had hitherto to be said by pictures or symbols could now be expressed, much more succinctly and quickly, in a few characters. This is one explanation. Another that has been put forward is that these written characters are messages that someone has left for a friend.

The Libyco-Berber characters can be read, and all those in the Grand Kabylie have been transliterated. One fairly long legend reads "ZDZRBNIG." No one has ventured to make sense of any of the inscriptions, which is all the more provoking in that not merely do the Touaregs use an almost identical script today in the form of the Tifnar characters, but inscriptions in this lost language are scattered all over the cave paintings of the Tassili. There can be little doubt that if the inscriptions are ever read, they will give a very good inkling into the mysteries of rock art.

TASSILI-N-AJJER

The Tassili mountains are a sandstone plateau, one of the most westerly in the Central Sahara, standing at a height of about three-thousand-feet. Erosion has crumbled the wedding-cake shape of the original rock formation into numerous *oueds* or canyons that run from north to south, often developing a diagonal bend to the east. There are many upstanding columns of sandstone, now detached from the parent plateau, which have resisted the erosive effect of the wind and which advance like the scouts of an oncoming army of crags toward the spectator. The free-standing columns and bastions of uneroded rock harbor numerous rock shelters.

At the bottom of the valleys springs permeate through the porous sandstone and form perpetual pools of water — a very rare sight in the Sahara. In the pools live catfish, and even dwarf crocodiles. These spring-fed natural reservoirs provide water for the vegetation that turns the Tassili into a perpetual oasis. It is as well to stress this favorable aspect of the place, because it is forbidding enough — so forbidding that it is almost impossible to believe that it was once the center of a flourishing agricultural civilization, with pastures overspread with forest trees and echoing to the sound of lowing beeves and the belling of hounds led out by hunters to the chase of the great animals of the jungle who harbored hard by.

The Tassili has, in fact, suffered from a progressive drying out process. This has been the lot of the Sahara as a whole. The first arrivals here were Neolithic men belonging to the African culture. They were hunters who arrived around 6800 B.C. around the same time the hunters and herdsmen of the Grand Kabylie tribe were creating their paintings. At that time, the whole of the Sahara was a lush savannah land like the present Niger valley.

Through some cataclysm of nature, perhaps the northward shift of the ice cap, the whole climate began to change and become progressively drier. It is difficult to be sure when this came about. Lajoux found cattle bones that he dated between 3250 and 2950 B.C. Cooke felt that the Sahara continued in its fertile period until approximately 2700 B.C. He established this date by refence to a deposit of guano in the Hoggar, now a vast area to the southeast of the Tassili. The Rudners, on the other hand, felt that dessication around 2000 B.C. and that the Tassili paintings were created between 3080 and 1200 B.C. What happened to the survivors of the dessication process?

With the drying up of their feeding grounds, some beasts (deer, for example) trotted off on the road to extinction. Others, elephant, rhinoceros, and giraffe, may have trekked south to join the main herds in greener pastures. Did the Tassili herdsmen painters stay behind to develop into the Berber or Fulani people or did they adapt themselves to a drier way of life and move across the desert southward? Observers have pointed out that the Bushman, though a very recent arrival in the Kalahari desert, seems to be well adapted to desert conditions. He has skin folds around his eyes to protect him from glare and driven sand, a small wiry frame ideal for hard going in desert country, and a reserve store of energy in the shape of his steatopygous bottom, which, it is claimed, serves the same function as a camel's hump. I shall try to suggest elsewhere that the faces in some of the Tassili paintings are Bushmanoid rather than simian. They have usually been interpreted to be animal masks.

In order to see what life used to be like in this part of Africa it is necessary to climb to the top of the plateau above Djanet. Here, the best of the paintings are to be found. They fall into four main classes that correspond to the periods at which they were executed.

First comes the period of the disk-headed or blob-headed men, who are often called "aniconic," meaning faceless. Here is one of the recurring taboos of rock art, the refusal to represent human features.

A charming female portrait at Tin Teferiest has her hair pulled back over her head with threads to form a pattern. At the edge of the pattern the painter has stopped and the interior is a blank. Hair styles involving tufts of hair pulled back by threads are still used by African girls who do not have a thick growth of hair, and the Bushmen and the Hottentots, whose hair grew in "peppercorns" or small isolated tufts, treated theirs in the same way. Miniature figures, which may represent babies and, thus, an unspoken prayer for children, cover the figure of the girl. Were they added when she was painted, or later?

Not all the figures are aniconic, or rendered naturally. There are plenty of "matchstick" or filiform men who appear in virtually every painting school of rock art, and who are here shown hurrying to the pursuit of game, rhinoceroses, elephants, and a buffalo called *Bubalus antiquus*. They are assisted by packs of hounds. Sometimes, the figures are not faceless, but given weird visages that most observers have chosen to treat as masks, and suggested to be a connection between the rock paintings and the art of Black Africa today. There is no clear proof that the gesticulating figures are masked dancers, however. They could well be mythological paintings like the giant god of Jabberen, who is eighteen feet high. Another great god, at Sefar, is surrounded by women at prayer. Men and women, who are sometimes impossible to distinguish from one another, have an apricot skin color that recalls that of the Bushmen. The men carry weapons that recall those of ancient Egypt, bows, arrows, and throwing sticks.

Besides portraying aniconic men and women, the artists of the early period of Tassili painted the abundant wildlife of the region, which included giraffes and hippopotamuses. There have certainly not been any hippo in the country for a very long time. The largest of the dwarf crocodiles to be caught in the oasis pools was only seven feet long.

Later, probably much later, because, according to African farmers at least, game and stock do not mix well, came the paintings of the pastoralist period. Wild animals still appear, but they are overshadowed by cattle and sheep. The cows are attractively dappled in blotched red, white, white and grey, and fawn and white. Of course, there is no way of knowing whether these were their true colors, but it has been suggested that the fact that they were dappled at all indicates the result of centuries of domestication and inbreeding. The cattle do not have humps like the modern cattle of Africa did before the arrival of the whites.

The men in the paintings now seem darker. They carry accessories that suggest Black Africa. There are many peaceful themes, including mother-and-child scenes with vignettes of stock rearing, herding, and hunting.

Cutting across this Saharan idyll comes the thunder of the wheels of war chariots. Horses with chariots and armed riders, like the Cyrenaican amazon who was beheaded by Theron at Saguntum, appear in large numbers. Are they the reflection of things seen by the painters themselves, or, as has been conjectured, the work of far-traveled foreign mercenaries? It has even been suggested that there were never any chariots at Tassili at all. They are merely copies of cult chariots associated with the worship of the gods.

The preoccupation with war and weapons of war (though chariots did have peaceful uses as well) does, however, seem to reflect some kind of upheaval. Do these scenes portray the invasion of the Sahara by people such as the Cretans who fought against Rameses III of Egypt in Libya around 1250?

As the pastoralist period comes to an end, it seems useful to attempt to sum up some of its more important aspects. The pastoralists have been more inclined to reveal themselves in their art than earlier generations of painters. They have copper-colored bodies, hair that hangs straight but is usually held in by a snood or headdress, and wear loin cloths. Some of the faces in the frescoes seem to be Hamitic, and look like modern Somalis, others could have stepped straight from an Egyptian tomb painting, and some seem markedly Negro or Negroid. There are also undoubted Caucasoids among the many protraits on the shelter walls.

Henri Lhote, whose expedition of 1956-7 revealed so much of the riches of Tassili, postulated that there had been at least two waves of development in painting. One, associated with the pastoralists, had been inspired by white people related to prehistoric Europeans of the Cro-Magnon type (whose remains have been found in other parts of North Africa). The earlier round-headed and masked figures were related to Black Africa.

Though great weight must be attached to Lhote's views, they have not always found favor with his fellow countrymen. I myself feel that Tassili was an oasis town like Kano today or the Turfan oasis in China during the dark ages. Men and women of all types were to be seen there, and as at Turfan, their presence in the paintings may depend on the degree to which they were involved in worship. Nor must one forget that skin color is rarely a realistic impression in antiquity. Men in Egyptian and Etruscan frescoes are always rendered in dark red, women in white or light colors.

The penultimate stage of Tassili painting is called the "cameline," because the camel, though it seems so adjusted to life in the Sahara, is a late arrival there. Humped zebu cattle are also to be seen, and these, too, are an indication of comparative modernity because they were introduced from Arabia during the Semitic migrations. Besides domestic animals the wild fauna of the desert are shown as well, those being gazelles, ostriches, oryxes, and goats.

The cameline period stretches on until our own day, for the Touaregs of the desert, little troubled with the iconoclasm that characterizes other Muslims, portray themselves on the shelter walls, on camels, or horses equipped with Arab stirrups. The latest paintings by the men of Tassili are disappointing. There is a coarseness and lack of invention about them, while commentators have not been slow to point out that the act of love, depicted with grace and sympathy in the early period, has degenerated into obscenity in the latter one. Besides the feeling of being inhabitants of a doomed oasis that must have grown on the Tassilians as the rate of dessication increased, with a consequent lowering of their morale and their will to paint, the discovery of writing had superceded painting, as it had in Kabylie. Scrawled Libyco-Berber inscriptions replace the elaborate and graceful paintings of the past.

The mystery that hangs over much of the Tassili paintings is deepened by the lack of archaeological excavations to provide the necessary background to the art by an investigation of the men who painted them. Paradoxically, not just Tassili but the whole of the Sahara is strewn with rock tools and weapons. Guide books to the region beg visitors not to pick them up and take them away, as so many tourists have done in the past. The arid nature of the soil makes extensive archaeological digging so difficult as to be almost impossible.

The lack of an archaeological background is all the more to be regretted in that Tassili is the knot that ties the civilizations of the Mediterranean to ancient Egypt and to the much less sophisticated rock painters of the south and center of Africa. Did any of the inhabitants of the Tassili region stray south, and stay long enough to be portrayed on the frescoes of the Brandberg?

The possibilities of recognizing racial types at Tassili becomes fainter as the painters now begin to represent the human figure by two triangles whose apexes touch. Nevertheless, great skill and finesse continue to be shown in the rendering of the details of dress, weapons, and horse trappings.

ETHIOPIA

Rock paintings of great interest have been discovered in Ethiopia at Genda Bifton, Sourre, forty miles southwest of Dire Dawa, at Lago Oda, about fourteen miles away from Sourre, and in the Cave of the Wild Boar, near Dire Dawa, as well as north of Harar.

They fall into two main series, the earlier showing herdsmen with dress and weapons resembling the modern-day Hamite tribes of the region, accompanied by unhumped cattle that must be more than two-thousand years old. The early paintings are executed in a style that recalls that of the Sahara.

In the later paintings, humped Zebu cattle appear, alongside camels. The camel is a very convenient animal for dating pictures, and these later paintings may be assumed to belong to the Greco-Roman era.

The output of paintings in the early series is impressive. At Lago Oda, there is a frieze of nearly a thousand figures stretching for forty-five yards. They include unhumped cattle, elephants, rhinoceros, buffalo, lions, hyenas, antelope, and giraffe. A series of schematic paintings overlies the early naturalistic ones. Genda Bifton has paintings in a sequence that begins with yellow, then black, pale red, red-brown, yellow, red, and black. Longhorn cattle, antelopes, cheetah, and buffalo can be distinguished, along with men carrying bows and wearing combs.

In one Ethiopian shelter — the Cave of the Wild Boar — the later series of paintings are represented. They depict elephants, antelope buffalo, lion, and other large carnivores. At another shelter at Harar, there are friezes of longhorn cattle, hunters shooting ostriches, and jackals. There are also paintings of the imprints of human feet.

THE SUDAN

There are several rock painting sites in the Sudan, notably northern Darfur, but the painting site *par excellence* is in the Dajo Hills in Southern Darfur. Here, hundreds of black and red paintings have been discovered, some showing elephants, giraffes, and antelope, others infantry and cavalry carrying shields and spears. Since the horse only reached the Sudan about 1000 B.C., the paintings are certainly not older than that date, and they may be much later because one of the horses is clad in padded armor, a protection worn by both horses and their riders in the Empire of Bornu in the Sudan when it was visited by Clapperton in the early nineteenth century.

TANZANIA

Just as Tanzania partakes both of the dry nature of the Horn of Africa and the greener game pastures of the south, so the paintings in this area are a bridge between the naturalistic styles of both north and south.

Naturalistic and schematic paintings occur side by side in the thousands of pictures that have now been recorded from Tanzania. Many of the best of these are to be found in about a hundred principal sites. Some of the earliest work takes the form of monochrome animals, which become more detailed, then enter a final phase of extreme stiffness with thick outlines. Schematic figures appear quite early, some of them being paintings of animals in which the rendering of the outline becomes so conventionalized

These humans with animal heads may represent
hunters who have donned animal masks as a trophy
of the chase, or they may originate in the abundant
mythology of Old Africa. (Courtesy Ministry of
National Education, Tanzania.)

Chief Shangali admiring rock paintings at Kondoa, Tanzania. (Photo Courtesy Tanzanian National Tourist Board.)

Rock painting at Kondoa, Tanzania, showing a giraffe. (Photo Courtesy Tanzania National Tourist Board.)

that identity is only recognizable by some feature that is caricatured, such as the neck in a giraffe.

Some sites are particularly notable. Kisana, on the eastern edge of the Iramba plateau, contains paintings of ostriches, giraffes, antelopes, elands, and a dog. Kondoa has many badly preserved paintings on slabs of the metamorphic rock that makes up the small hill there. The paintings show elephants, humans, and giraffes.

Another interesting site is Ilongero. Here a hill was taboo to the local inhabitants. It had never been climbed, but when an archaeologist persuaded the chief to accompany him in an official visit to the top they were rewarded by the sight of an overhanging rock seventy feet long and nine feet high that was completely covered with paintings. The pictures, in red, depicted giraffes, antelopes, an elephant, and possibly a leopard and a hyena as well.

Cheke and Kisese have proved very rewarding sites, yielding animal and human figures in a rich variety of colors. Interesting scenes depict a trapped elephant, dancers, and a female rhinoceros pursuing the male — the normal method of rhinoceros courtship. The sequence of the paintings at Kisese and Cheke, as worked out by Dr. Leakey, is of red animals, purple humans and animals, outline drawings of animals, outline figures in black, claret animals that are finely drawn, badly drawn claret red animals, animals in a thick red outline stiffly drawn, conventionalized red-brick animals and badly drawn orange humans and animals. The sequence of the group of cave

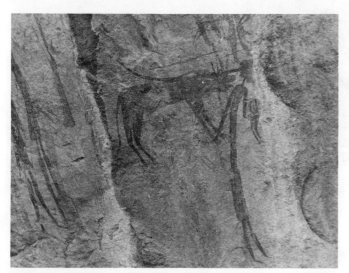

This hunter from Tanzania wears an elaborate head-dress. (Photo Courtesy Ministry of National Education, Tanzania.)

paintings at Mungoni wa Kolo is completely different.[3]

If the animals are not always easy to identify, the symbols are invariably so obscure as to daunt even the most daring from trying to interpret them at all. They have been compared at one time or another to sun symbols, stylized drawings of kraals or kopjes, or, if they take the form of the usual assemblages of dots and dashes, it has been claimed that they are either psychological dream patterns or the ideographs of a lost language.

Rock engravings are very scarce, though some renderings of animals do occur. "Cup and ring" engravings have been recorded, but since they occur on the stones of a building, they are outside the present survey.

KENYA

Kenya is a very recent country, so far as the discoveries of rock paintings are concerned, but it is to be hoped that many more, as yet, undiscovered examples will be brought to light. There are many crude white daubings, apparently the recent work of the Masai, but the most important site so far is at Tweedies' Shelter on Mount Elgon, about fifteen miles north of Kitale, in the middle of a buffalo- and elephant-haunted forest. The least exposed wall of this shelter is covered by paintings that run in the form of a frieze around the cave. They are carried out in red or white, or red and white. Others are painted much higher up, in an alcove fifteen feet above the floor. Because the paintings represent unhumped cattle, they presumably date back to between 1000 B.C. to A.D. 100, the dates for the dominance of the unhumped as opposed to the humped Zebu, which are given by Childe.

Not merely are the herds of Mount Elgon domesticated cattle, they also appear to be the product of an intensive grazing industry because their udders are well developed while their horns are apparently artificially deformed, no doubt, to reduce the casualties in fights between bulls.

UGANDA

Like Kenya, Uganda is still not fully exploited as far as painting sites are concerned. Most of those

[3]Cole, *The Prehistory of East Africa*, p. 234.

which have come to light so far are realistic paintings in red.

At Nyiro Rock in the Teso area, geometric designs overlay red naturalistic paintings. The realistic paintings are of humans, and also of acacia pods and canoes, rather unusual subjects. One of the canoes is seven feet long, a large size for a rock painting. It is significant that the local tribe, the Iteso, regard Nyiro as a shrine, and preserve the tradition that the paintings were carried out by people with lighter skins than themselves, no doubt Bushmen. The Iteso make offerings at the Nyiro Rock to obtain rain.

Next to Nyiro the principal site of interest in Uganda is Lolui Island on Lake Victoria. A large boulder and some supporting boulders form a small shelter, and on the underside of its roof are geometric paintings, chiefly concentric circles and dumbbells, in different shades of red, with one naturalistic painting of a sailing canoe.

MALAWI AND ZAMBIA

There is more of a connection between Malawi and Zambia than there is between the two countries and Rhodesia. The two countries seem to have influenced one another. They do not seem to have influenced Rhodesia as much as they have been influenced by it.

Malawi and Zambia differ considerably, the former being a country where the lush vegetation of the Shire valley moves into the ever-verdant lakeside plains that run up to the escarpment. Further north, the rolling plateau of the Dedza and Mchinji areas was once covered entirely with woodland, broken with granite kopjes and ranges that contain the painting sites.

In Zambia, too, well-wooded and watered country is interspersed with kopjes and ridges and damp dambos containing a stream or spring, dambos that sometimes contain relics of the tropical evergreen forest that has now disappeared. Africa, as Livingstone once remarked, is a country of dried-up rivers and streams, tokens of the damper climate that it once enjoyed. Yet, parts of Malawi must have changed comparatively little since the days of the hunter artists. In some areas, such as the headwaters of the Likwenu, it is possible to find undiscovered

In Africa, water is life. It is not surprising, then, that many rock paintings sites are associated with rivers that drew game to them, such as the great Victoria Falls, which constitute a great magnet for game, especially during the dry season. (Photo Courtesy Zambian National Tourist Bureau.)

Many paintings, such as these in this Malawian cave, are placed so high that painting them must have caused considerable trouble for the artists. One reason that they are placed so high may have been that their influence would have a longer "range." (Photo Courtesy Malawi Tourist Board.)

rock shelters, all of which hold, at least, the promise of undiscovered paintings or engravings. Most of these have, alas, been almost continually tenanted since the time of the rock painters. So troubled has life been in Malawi that, until the arrival of Sir Harry Johnston in the latter half of the nineteenth century, there can rarely have been a generation when someone was not sheltering in the caves, as fugitives from the Yaos, the Ngoni, or some other invader. Constant use of the caves may have tended to obliterate many paintings and account for the low number that have been found in Malawi.

Both Malawi and Zambia must have been good hunting country before the rise of the present-day heavy population with their slash-and-burn cultivation methods. On the plateaux, forty-foot trees formed a continuous ceiling with their intertwined branches preventing the growth of undercroft, so that hunters could weave freely among the trees. Wild fruits and edible roots abound over the whole area, enough to support tribes of primitive hunters today. These were supplemented by abundant game in the past.

In Zambia and Malawi, the shelter painters sought out rock surfaces in the old sandy quartzes of the Basement System that form ridges, escarpments, or kopjes. This rock system contains an abundance of shelters. Further south, on the Inangwa and Lake Malawi watershed, granites were chosen on which to paint as they were in Rhodesia. As was the case everywhere in Africa, only a few of the available rock surfaces were used, and these were overpainted again and again. Painting sites tend to be concentrated in lower caves near the base of the hills, which often show signs of occupation, or in higher shelters well up on the sides of the hills.

Possibly because they form a narrow bottleneck between the tsetse-free areas north and south, the two countries have formed a barrier to the spread of the style of naturalistic rock painting found to the north and south of them. With a very few exceptions the rock paintings in the area are almost all schematic and abstract. While painted pregnant antelopes and a lion from Malawi have been recorded and, while many of the abstracts are obviously schematized animals such as snakes, the typical Zambian or Malawian painting is geometric.

Paintings of this sort, though characteristic of the area, are nonetheless clearly related to those to be found much farther north and south. They include "gridirons" in black or red paint, ladders and circles in red, ovals of red or claret made up of dots, concentric circles, designs that look like hairpins, crescents, "tectiform" designs and parallel lines that form a "U."

Other paintings are much more complicated. One looks like a house roof in process of construction, another has been fittingly compared to a comet, while others are so involved that they suggest plans or diagrams. One very large painting, possibly the largest abstract ever painted in Africa, occurs at Mpunzi Mountain, in the northern region. The world *Mpunzi*

These "formlings" may represent stars. From the Mlanda Cave, Ncheu district, Malawi. (Photo Courtesy Malawi Tourist Agency.)

106

has been derived from *kupunzire*, meaning "to learn," suggesting that the mountain may have been a place of initiation or for the teaching of some secret ritual.

The painting is eight feet long and starts five feet above the ground. The ambiguity of the design has been heightened by the fading of the red paint in which the picture was created. Its form is such that some have declared that it is related to the "Mantis" pictures supposedly made by Bushmen in South Africa, while others have declined to be able to see in them any resemblance to a Mantis at all.

Another Malawian painting site, the shelter on Chencherre hill, north of Dedza, is of particular interest because it not only contains the usual strange abstracts, concentric circles, and a gridiron in red, but, until, recently it was also used as a wardrobe for a local *vinyau* secret society, who kept their split cane costumes in it.

Mwalawolemba shelter on Mikalongwe Hill has already been referred to in the introduction. The abstract motifs that it contains can be found in other shelters, along with crudely drawn "star" designs.

Observers have seen in the Malawian and Zambian paintings a sequence in which the earlier pictures of animals in silhouettes, with naturalistic paintings of animals that are sometimes pregnant, are followed by crudely drawn human figures. Then follows finger painting, overlaid by some fine naturalistic paintings at the end. The paintings have been assumed to be the work of Stone Age peoples of the Nachikufuan Culture, an archaeological level that lasted for a long time and went through three distinct stages. While no firm dates seem to have been arrived at for Malawian paintings, middens below the painted friezes in Zambia have been dated by the radio carbon method to between 5590 and 2880 B.C.

The problem of why Malawi and Zambia contain

Rock paintings at Chenchegrere, Dedza District. (Photo Courtesy Malawi Tourist Board.)

Red and white paintings from Mukoma, Kefete, Zambia. The symbol at the top of the picture has often been compared to a comet. (Photo Courtesy Zambia Tourist Board.)

abstract paintings, with hardly any examples of the naturalistic school to be found to the north and south of them, in Tanzania and Rhodesia, has never been really convincingly explained, though it has been argued either that the naturalistic paintings are the work of a particular race who were absent, or at least not present in very large numbers, in this part of central Africa. Either that or Malawi and Zambia belong to a "Schematic School Belt," which stretches right across Africa from east to west.[4]

RHODESIA

Part of the rock painting wealth of Rhodesia is undoubtedly due to the fact that it has been thoroughly explored. Both the black and white inhabitants of the country show a strong local

[4] J. and I. Rudner, *The Hunter and His Art,* p. 226.

patriotism about their paintings and Mr. Creech, the Director of Photography there, told me how, on occasion, he had been directed to a completely unknown cave by the local folk.

The Matopos Hills, near Bulawayo, constitute typical Rhodesian painting country. Here a small, smooth, round-topped hill has been capped by several giant, round granite boulders. These dome-shaped hills rise above the surrounding woodland and dominate the view, which Cecil Rhodes once described as "a view of the world." The spheroidal shape of the capping boulders is due to the process of exfoliation. The granite rocks are constantly losing their corners through the alternate heats and colds of day and night as the crust first warms and then cools quickly. The splitting off of the rock shells produces dome-shaped boulders nestling on top of one another, with clefts between the roofs and walls of which can be painted. The rocks offer textured surfaces that hold paint well and overhangs that protect the completed painting like a canopy.

All these factors were of extreme importance to the hunter artists, and they have made the Matopos the great gallery of central African rock art.

The ridge of the Matopos rises about nine-hundred feet above lush green valleys, at an elevation of five-thousand feet. Because the rainfall is much heavier than in southern Africa, the cover and browsing for game is much richer. In the clefts between the granite domes and the deep valleys which intersect them flourish kaffirboom, Cape Chestnuts, acacias, euphorbias, and tree ferns. Bright lichens on the granite boulders supply nourishment for small game like lizards, while bigger game such as elephant, hippo, lion, crocodile, giraffe, rhino, buffalo, eland, wildebeest, kudu, zebra, leopard, baboon, monkeys, and pythons all made the area their home. Some of this abundant fauna has now disappeared, but there is an abundant record of them on the rocks.

The whole area is charged with a feeling of commemoration. First it was a shrine to the Matabele, because of the rain cult of Mlimo, which was brought to the Njile Cave five-hundred years ago by a priest of Mlimo who moved it from its previous residence in Zimbabwe, another granite citadel associated with cave paintings. Offerings of grain, bullocks, and beer were made to Mlimo to ensure an abundant

The Manemba Cave, Mtoko District, Rhodesia, is rich in distorted and semihuman figures, often with animal heads. (Photo Courtesy Rhodesian National Tourist Board.)

Paintings in the Rhodes Matopos National Park on the walls of the Silogwane Cave. (Photo Courtesy Rhodesian Ministry of Information.)

rainfall, while to the sound of the drum, sacred dances were carried out by young girls, who threw water into the air to induce rain by sympathetic magic.

In 1893, the power of Mlimo was put to the test. His priests said that the god had ordered that all the Europeans should be driven out and had promised victory. The Matabele rose but were defeated. A little later, the Mashona, the subject race over whom the Matabele had domineered, and who were also worshippers of Mlimo, rose and were also defeated.

Instead of being a sanctuary to the now discredited rain god, the Matopos became a shrine to the leader of the white Rhodesians, Cecil Rhodes, and the Shangani Patrol, settler volunteers who had been killed in the struggle after an epic battle with the Matabele. So the Matopos had a long history of sanctity, and great deeds, as the scenes of armed conflict pictured on the caves showed. Certainly not the least of those deeds was the courageous journey that Rhodes himself had made, unarmed, and with only three companions, to meet the *indunas* of the revolting Matabele and make peace with them.

The Matopos, in fact, is a type example of the continuing idea of sanctity associated with an area that contains rock paintings. Remains in the caves and shelters show an almost unbroken occupation from the Stone Age down to 1893. First, the Karanga hid there to escape from the Matabele, then the Matabele themselves took refuge from the whites.

Zimbabwe, which I have already mentioned, is another area of long associations. At Zimbabwe, engravings of animal spoor were followed by paintings, which in turn were followed by the building of the temple at Zimbabwe, a temple that has become the best-known shrine in Africa.

110

As has already been noticed, the types and subjects of Rhodesian painting cover a wide range. In the Domboshawa Cave, for example, early outlines of large animals can be seen, with a frieze of lively hunters brandishing bows and arrows superimposed on them. The hunters are portrayed in quite a naturalistic way, but close to them are matchstick men with exaggeratedly long legs superimposed on the old outline of a rhinoceros.

Domboshawa also illustrated giant-sized handprints, a ceremony in which strangely garbed figures appear to scatter water from containers — recalling the rain-making ceremonies associated with Mlimo, and pictures of sprouting roots — a rather unusual theme, as well as many more motifs.

Pictures on top of pictures again appear in the Makumbe Cave. Here, above a thirty-foot-long frieze of six elephants and their young walking in procession (just as they still do nowadays when visiting the water hole, according to African artists who love to portray these processions of elephants on the length of a tusk) are no fewer than fifteen superimposed layers. Over the silhouette of an elephant stalk many graceful animals that have been added at various times: small elephants, baboons, buffalo, and antelopes. So rich are the overpaintings that massed motifs occur again and again, as, for example, at Carolina Farm in Robert McIlwaine National Park. Here, large fishes of the bottlenose type are combined with men, formlings, antelopes, an elephant, and other strange creatures whose bodies are made up in large areas of dashes that perhaps symbolize rain. The

A closer look at some of the elephants that have given the Charewa Cave its name. (Photo Courtesy Rhodesian Ministry of Information.)

111

Why did the cave painters position their frescoes so high up on the cave walls? The Elephant Cave, Mwera Reserve, Rhodesia. (Photo Courtesy Rhodesian Ministry of Information.)

same park provides scenes of crocodile hunts, animals trapped between rocks, tree- and boulder-strewn scenes and other landscape paintings. Elsewhere, at Kisanzi Farm, Darwendale, sprightly kudu scamper past what might conceivably be a net.

One of the strangest assembly of scenes is to be found at Diana's Vow Farm, Rusape. Here a giant sorcerer, garbed in a jackal mask and head trappings, lies at full length, spilling his seed onto the ground, while below him Lilliputian men dance superimposed over animals or take part in what appears to be a bottle party. Other weird creatures with heads like scorpions and skeletonized bats' wings caper over a camel. At Glen Norah are more strange creatures, "crocodile men," whose appearance must certainly have terrified those who first beheld them.

Varied as are the motifs of the paintings it is possible to group almost every example into the following schema: animal paintings, hunting scenes, including confrontations with game and its disposal among the hunting party, dead or wounded animals, predators hunting, a few domestic animals such as the sheep and dog, snakes, mythical animals' family scenes, including the "mother and child" theme, scenes of war and palavers, caricatures where the subject is treated playfully, people going about their daily business or engaged in some ceremony or walking or dancing.

Racial types are rather difficult to distinguish among the paintings. There is a man with a prognothaus jaw at Ruchera Cave who, had he been discovered further south, would have been declared

The difficulties of interpreting paintings are increased when they are overlaid with growths of lichen, such as those examples from the Charewa Elephant Cave in Rhodesia. (Photo Courtesy of Rhodesian Ministry of Information.)

This painting from Robert Mcilwaine National Park, near Salisbury, Rhodesia, shows a figure apparently chopping down a tree with a stone axe. (Photo Courtesy Rhodesian Ministry of Information.)

The problems of interpretation are well illustrated by this Rhodesian painting. It depicts human figures, decorated with dots, stripes, and headdresses, and masked. Above them is laid out their equipment, baskets, skins, bows, quivers, staves, and edible roots. This is a fragment of a larger scene that included a large reclining figure, with a small woman, a chicken, dogs, a snake, and more humans. Interpretations have varied. Some have seen the picture as the burial of a king, while others have interpreted it as an encounter between two different cultures. (Courtesy Rhodesian Ministry of Information.)

A frieze of game in a cave at Mtoko, Rhodesia. (Photo Courtesy Rhodesian Ministry of Information.)

to have been a "Bergdama." There is also a very negroid looking man from Rakodze Farm, Marandellas.

Observers have not hesitated to interpret particular groups of figures as people who are engaged in a specific activity. Thus Elizabeth Goodall, the great expert on Mashonaland paintings, has seen, in some of the pictures, medicine men picking edible roots, anthropomorphic creatures, crocodile people, primeval mothers' cave ghosts, burial ceremonies and funeral services, rain goddesses, rain ceremonies, rain sacrifices, and trees of life.

Witch doctors did not exist among the Bushmen, and therefore, they may not have existed among the early hunter artists either, otherwise many of Mrs. Goodall's conjectures sound plausible enough.[5] Even

[5] See the whole of the section "Rock Paintings of Mashonaland," in E. Goodall, C.K. Cooke, and J. Desmond Clark's *Prehistoric Rock Art of the Federation of Rhodesia and Nyasaland*, pp. 3-111.

she, however, is baffled by many of the subjects that are represented. These include curious round motifs, made up of tiny white dashes enclosed within dark "balloons," with two of the enclosing balloons merging with one another. Do the white dashes represent raindrops and the meeting and mingling of the two balloons show the familiar sight of two rain clouds being blown apart with streamers of cloud stretching between them?

There are also various geometric patterns, some of them maze shaped, some which are more graphics. However these motifs are to be interpreted, there can be little doubt that their profusion, number, and diversity of style represent an activity continued throughout generations.

Though the paintings of Rhodesia are so diverse, an attempt has been made to group them all into six distinct styles.

First come simple outline drawings of animals, all in one color, which stand stiffly by themselves and

115

These paintings, in the Manemba Cave, Mtoko, Rhodesia, are part of a 150-foot frieze. (Photo Courtesy Rhodesian Ministry of Information.)

A general view of the Charewa, or Elephant Cave, in Rhodesia. (Photo Courtesy Rhodesian Ministry of Information.)

Another part of the weird and puzzling frieze of the Manemba Cave, Rhodesia. (Photo Courtesy Rhodesian Ministry of Information.)

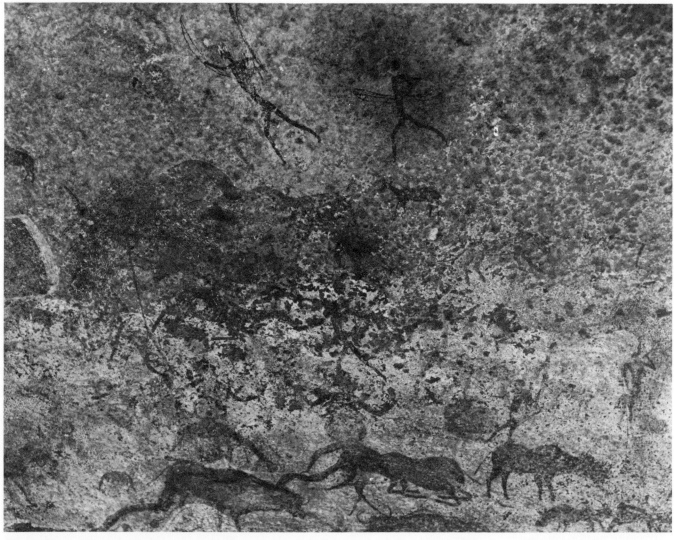

Another section of the frieze from the Charewa Cave. (Photo Courtesy Rhodesian Ministry of Information.)

which are accompanied by "matchstick" figures. Then there are single color outlines, with the interior sometimes only partly filled in, together with human figures that show some grouping and modeling. Outline drawings with detailed rendering of animals come next, together with human figures that, though detailed, do not have recognizable faces.

Animals follow, drawn in a naturalistic style and rendered either in one color or in a combination of one or more. This category includes groups of human figures, with landscapes, mystic beings, and complex schematic designs. This is the "Golden Age" of Rhodesian rock art. Then there follows degenerate charcoal or white paintings of circles and spirals that are the crude attempts of later comers of Iron Age times to imitate and emulate the "old master" drawings of the past. Lastly, there are white figures, drawn on a very large scale and painted inside the line with kaolin clay. Again, these drawings are considered to be the degenerate and imitative attempts to equal the master drawings of the past.

Like all sequences, this lies open to two objections. The first is that the discovery of just one new cave might upset the classification arrived at hitherto. Secondly, it is difficult to see why rock art should have evolved in just such a way as this sequence suggests.

Dates ranging from 7450 B.C. for Pomongwe Cave in the Matopos, to 2350 B.C. Amadzimba Cave, also in the Matopos, have been suggested. Other late Rhodesian paintings are as recent as 20 B.C. They all correspond to the Rhodesian Later Stone Age, which is represented in Mashonaland by a cultural level known as Wilton, and the counterpart culture, Pomongwan, in Matabeleland.

THE DRAKENSBERG

This classic painting site lies in a range of mountains that stretch some six-hundred miles from the Transvaal to the Cape. It is divided by the boundary line between South Africa and the independent African state of Lesotho.

The Afrikaans' name for the range means "Dragon Mountains," either because of a legend of a dragon that, in former days, was supposed to roam the mountain or because the upraised peaks of the Drakensberg could be compared fancifully to the scales along the ridge of a dragon's spine. The Zulu word for the mountain complex is even more evocative. It is *Quathlamba,* meaning "barrier of upwarding pointing spears."

The Drakensberg is not a free-standing mountain range but the escarpment on the edge of a plateau, an escarpment that runs in a roughly wedge-shaped mass from Royal Natal Park to Coleford Nature Reserve. At the point of the wedge is Giant's Castle Game Reserve, which contains many of the finest paintings. The height of the escarpment averages around nine-thousand feet for about one-hundred miles of its range. The Great "Mont aux Sources," or "Mountain of Springs," is the Continental Divide of South Africa. Two rivers rise here within just a few miles of one another, the Khubedu, which turns into the Orange river and flows right across the continent into the Atlantic, and the Tugela, which flows over the escarpment to become one of the highest waterfalls in the world, and run eastward into the Indian Ocean.

The Drakensberg is a geological canvas prepared by nature for the brush of the cave painter. Where the crags at the edge of the escarpment now raise their needlelike points, crags with picturesque names such as Amphitheatre, Cathedral Peak, Windsor Castle, and The Rhino, a sea flowed in remote geological times. Millions of years passed, during which its waters laid down the sedimentary layers of the Karoo System. About 150 million years ago, Gondawanaland, one of the big geological formations of the area, broke up, and as the face of the earth cracked under great stress, molten lava poured out through the fissures and exploded as it met the sea water.

The layer of basaltic lava laid down in the eruption was some thirty-six hundred yards in thickness, but erosion has now worn most of it away and it appears to the eye of the visitor in the shape of the surviving basalt masses, spiky crags that lift themselves up from the edge of the escarpment.

Underneath the layer of basalt is the cave sandstone, eroded on the outside and honeycombed within, with caves where acid-carrying water has eaten away the stone.

In many of these caves lived the last of the Bushmen. They were quite selective about their homes and liked to choose those caves which turned away from the wet season rains that fall between January and March.

Stray members of the Bushman nation had undoubtedly lived in the Drakensberg before the advance of the Boers and the Bantu made all the survivors take refuge there (except for the frequently

Scene from the Battle Cave, Drakensberg, Natal, South Africa, depicting warriors with bows and arrows, and a casualty who has gashed his arm to promote the flow of blood and thus escape the effects of the poisoned arrow that caused the wound. (Photo Courtesy South African Tourist Agency.)

The Bushmen were inveterate cattle thieves. What they could not carry off they killed. Here, vengeance is at hand as an impi of Zulus or Matabele appear on the horizon. From Wood. (Photo by Stella Mayes Reed.)

mentioned remnant that went to the Kalahari). In the depleted numbers in which they now were, they could undoubtedly have sustained life in this area, without ever venturing out to raid the white man's cattle.

The territory abounds in game. Antelope, eland, mountain reedbuck, rhebuck, duikers, bushbuck, klipspringers, hyrax, and baboons are all to be found in the Drakensberg as well as more than 170 different types of birds.

When the Bushmen were in residence, the area abounded in big game, as their paintings can testify. It did not take much to feed a Bushman. He could eat anything — a useful faculty in Africa even today — and if everything else in the way of nutriment failed him, he could have lived on the small game, such as lizards and snakes, and the wild fruits that abounded in this city of refuge.

Why were the Bushmen not permitted to live quietly in their last fortress? Partly, it was the racial hate felt for them by both whites and blacks, partly it was a desire on the part of the white men to carry off their wives and daughters as concubines, partly it was a fear that, left to themselves, the Bushmen would grow strong and become a menace again, for fear of the Bushmen was as strong among the blacks as it was in the whites, and a Matabele impi, who would have marched off the edge of a cliff if their commanding officer ordered them to, quailed before enemies armed with missiles so deadly that their touch would turn a strong healthy young man into a demented cretin, writhing in horrible death agonies. The act of the Bushmen that signed and sealed their death warrant was their persistence in cattle raids from the apparent safety of their stronghold in the Drakensberg. It is no exaggeration to say that if they had cut the throats of the wives and children of the Boers and the Bantu the latter would have borne them less ill will than for what they did do — to kill all the cattle that they could not carry off. "We soon forget the death of a father," says Machiavelli, "but the loss of our inheritance we remember for the rest of our lives." Cattle were life in old South Africa.

Why did the Bushmen persist in their raids? Not, I feel, because they needed the beef. There was plenty of other game that they could have caught. Not because, as Dorothea Bleek says, and everyone else has said after her, because they were deliberately carrying on a war of revenge against the whites who had shot their game or driven them away from the watering places that they regarded as theirs — if that had been the case, they would have made war on the whites but not the blacks because the amount of game killed by the Bantu by their primitive weapons was negligible. No, I feel they continued their raids because it was part of their way of life, and to abandon them would have been to admit the superiority of their enemies.

They must have known the consequences of their decision. In 1869 a Boer commando destroyed the last organized party of Bushmen in the Drakensberg. The Boer rifles could always outrange the puny bows of the little hunters. A few survivors (one of whom we shall meet toward the end of this book) lingered in the hill fortresses or dragged out their lives as bondsmen on neighboring farms until the turn of the century.

The somber story of the Bushmen cannot but throw a melancholy light over even the beauties of the Drakensberg, scenically the finest, as well as the most artistically rewarding, of all the painting sites of Africa. As might be expected from a watershed, the whole area is rich in streams and rivers, and in them grow lush grasses on which eland and other game love to browse. The painted caves are placed strategically within these hunting grounds and near to a running stream.

It is difficult to make a selection from the caves, of which there are at least seventy important ones, thirty-six of which are of particular significance. Even in area such as this, which has been gone through with a fine-toothed comb by the best archaeologists in Africa, there is, no doubt, plenty more that is just waiting to be discovered.

Sequentially, it has been suggested that the Drakensberg follow the same order of styles as those which are to be found in nearby Lesotho and perhaps in other parts of South Africa as well.

During the First Period, which is roughly assigned to before 1620, thin human figures and animals in reddish brown or maroon appear.

Then follow, during the Second Period, dating from 1620 to 1800, a varied group of subjects including animals in several colors with shaded bodies, Bantu warriors, and men engaged in peaceful occupations. The men are in reddish brown, black, or white, and they are accompanied by some very tall human figures who wear animal masks and who may, therefore, be sorcerers or hunters clad in their spoils. There are shaded animals in various colors and scenes supposedly of initiation.

Period Three, which supposedly dates from 1800 to 1830, possesses many colored paintings without shading, portrayed in paint that is still bright. Domestic cattle begin to replace the elands, the favorite beast of the second period. There are pictures of the Ngoni invaders who crossed the Drakensberg in the early nineteenth century, and a little later Europeans and their unhumped cattle appear, together with horses and wagons. The paint of this latter period is cruder and not so fast.

Because the Bushmen survived longer in the Drakensberg than they did in Lesotho there is a subperiod that portrays the deathbed of the Bushmen. British soldiers and Boer commandos charge across the cave walls in paintings that may date from as late as the 1870s.

Such is the framework of Bushman art in this, their farewell exhibition. It is difficult to select the best subjects. The elands, rhebuck, antelopes, kudu, writhing python, and dappled cattle are very good. So, too, are the human portraits: Bushman archers wrapped in karosses, with others carrying quivers and skin bags. Bushmen in battle line fire volleys of arrows, or execute a wild dance in animal masks, while others, gesticulating wildly, surround a monster cow that is either bleeding to death from the mouth or is perhaps one of the "rain cows" of mythology. A supposed "Mantis Man" is also put forward as a mythological picture. Buck-headed men march past, presumably hunters celebrating their success, since they cannot be wearing the buck heads as hunting disguises. Buck do not walk on two legs. Other figures clap their hands in a dance, or go out to work with digging sticks. Hordes of matchstick men, too elongated to be either Bushmen or Bantu, dart about in what looks for all the world like a blackboard lesson in elementary tactics.

Besides the pictures of the Bushmen themselves there are, as we have noticed, paintings of the deadly enemies of the little people, but these do not predominate, a sign that the doomed people had no morbid preoccupation with their approaching end. Bantu tribes hurry past, engaged in the *mfecane,* or in search of new pastures. Other Bantu hunters return from the field. Redcoated British cavalry gallop after elands, and other horses caracole into the paintings.

Foreshortening and perspective indicate a desire to experiment, or perhaps a slackening of the rules of traditional art as the end approached.

SOUTHWEST AFRICA

All the regions of rock art have their special contribution to make to the art of the African continent as a whole and the southwest of Africa is just as distinctive in its way as any other region.

It is the kind of mountainous terrain, funneled, with caves, that the painters needed to do their best work. Not merely is it watered by the Orange and Windhoek rivers, but the coastal plains enjoy a winter rainfall. However, the cold Benguela Current, which flows northward up from the Cape and ultimately from the Antarctic, ensures that evaporation is low and there are few rain clouds formed to be carried inward.

In consequence, the region north of the coast chain of mountains, called the Karoo, is a very arid one, and still further north comes the dry area of Nanaqualand, the Kalahari, a desert into which the last of the Bushmen have retired. The Kalahari Bushmen are supposed to be of different tribes than those which did the paintings of South Africa, but this is not completely certain.

The dry areas are by no means unpeopled. They are eminently suitable for antelope such as the springbok and oryx, while the cold water currents of the sea are greatly relished by the whales, seals, and other sea beasts occasionally figured as much by the rock engravers as by the painters. The strong current was a deterrent to Henry the Navigator's captains who were sent out in the fifteenth century with orders to circumnavigate Africa. In time, they steered clear of the Benguela completely. It may, however, have been a help to early navigators trying to round the Cape from the other direction. At all events, ships are figured in the rock paintings but whether they are Phoenician sailing vessels, Portuguese caravels, or Dutch fluyts, remains a matter of dispute.

In the aridity of southwest Africa, generally, the southwest Cape stands out as a sort of oasis. It has a Mediterranean climate, wet winters and hot summers. The Olifants river (the Afrikaans name means "Elephant's") provides permanent water. Before the arrival of the Europeans, dense vegetation covered the sheltered valleys that abounded in game.

Only a few cedars remain on the "Cedar Mountains," or Cedarberg, which lie to the east of the Oliphants, rising to well over five-thousand feet and keeping a crown of snow for most of the winter. On the slopes of the mountains facing the rivers are to be found the rock shelters that were the preferred "canvas" of the artists.

The light dove blue of the Table Mountain sandstone sets off admirably the paintings, most of which are executed in brown, red, or yellow. Who were the painters? It has been suggested[6] with some plausibility that they were not the later Bushmen, but the early Hottentot shepherds and herdsmen, folk who were in touch with both the "Strandlopers" or beachcombers of the coast who lived on shellfish, and the Namaquas who still inhabit the region and whose tall figures can be seen in the paintings.

Southwestern pictures show the usual unerring touch in hitting off the spirit of an animal that we find in other rock art. There are elephant hunts, rhinoceros and bush pigs on the move, bucks fighting, elands reclining, and processions of baboons. There are also pictures from the sea that occur nowhere else in Africa, whales and other sea monsters, a rakish canoe with a large crew, and a whole array of mysterious ships. Much less difficult to refer to a particular period than the ships, which could belong to any time from Hanno to Dirk van Riebeck, are the Europeans in modern dress, many of whose portraits contain an undeniable element of caricature. The artist has manfully tackled subjects that must have been entirely novel to him, wagons and horses in complicated harness. Nonetheless, it is noticeable that he has been able to inject much more verve into the mule teams than the wagons. One mule hangs his head dejectedly while another pricks up his ears with a truly mulish expression.

Other noteworthy southwest Cape subjects include handprints, some realistic, some stylized animal bodies with human legs, animal-headed men, mother and child groups, family scenes, and vivid battle pieces.

[6] By A.J. H. Goodwin in the foreword to *Rock Paintings of the South West Cape,* by Townley Johnson, Hyme Rabinowitz and Percy Sieff. (Cape Town, 1959), p. 7.

This rock painting, from the Blyde River Canyon Nature Reserve, South Africa, depicts antelope that include the varieties of roan, sable, tsessebe, and impala. (Photo Courtesy South African Tourist Board.)

Like the Drakensberg, the southwest Cape area offers a quick introduction to the whole field of rock art. Citrusdale, Clanwilliam, and Ceres, the towns closest to the best sites, are all within driving distance of Cape Town. Not merely the Cape but the whole of southwest Africa is rich in paintings and engravings, with the Brandberg leading as the best known of its galleries. This tumbled and still largely unexplored granitic mass lies in the Namib Desert. Its crags contain not merely the monuments of a vanished art but the remains of prehistoric men. The contemporary Bergdamas, whose craggy type of face some have recognized in the paintings, may have contributed to the art.

The subjects of some of the paintings at least were suggested by the big movements of people, which took place in this area. Migrant folk, who may have been akin to the modern Namaquas, brought with them long-tailed sheep that appear in many of the paintings and indicate their late date. The most famous portrait — which perhaps may also be that of a migrant — in this area is of course the *White Lady of the Brandberg*. Though she does suggest that rock art is a much traveled commodity that retained its "non-African" quality down to the last, her portrait is by no means the best of the Brandberg pictures. There are springbok and ostriches, driven by hunters armed with quivers and nets, black bowmen with apparently infibulated members, who have surrounded an eland riddled with arrows, lizard men engaging in a boxing match, and a very negroid hunter stalking past carrying a bow and arrows.

On other panels, skeletonized giraffes meet horned serpents, a wayfarer pauses by a euphorbia, while a hunter with a bow and arrows appears to be leading

123

along a domesticated zebra, and elsewhere files of girls decked out in ostrich-shell beads and other finery mince past.

Not content with setting the archaeological world by the ears over the White Lady, the Abbé Breuil did the same again in the Elephant Cave in the Erongo Mountains. He claimed that a white elephant that appears conspicuously in the cave was really a member of an extinct species, the Mastodons. Most observers would now feel that it is merely a badly drawn elephant. The rhinoceros and elephants of the Brandberg, the hippopotamuses of Great Spitzkoppe and other large game appear in arid areas that can never have known such beasts for hundreds of years. This part of Africa is arid land verging into desert. Has the climate changed dramatically here as it did in the Sahara, or was the cave painter able to carry the image of an animal in his mind for a long time and paint it far from where he had seen it?

The earliest date obtainable for southwest Africa is 3790 B.C., the latest 940 B.C. Not surprisingly a land that has been painted and engraved for so long has become very rich. This is another area that acts as a quick introduction to rock painting and engravings as well, for at Twyfelfontein, paintings and engravings occur side by side, a very rare occurrence.

BANDIAGARA

Though mention has been made of painters who are still at work, tribesmen who still ceremoniously repaint the old painted caves in their areas that they use as rainmaking shrines, it is very unusual to be able to point to a living school of rock painters. To show how very singular this school of art is, it is only necessary to add that it exists in west Africa, an area not favored, as has been seen, by the rock painters.

The Dogon are not hunters, but farmers who grow millet. Hunting is only carried on for sport, and the formal religion of the tribe centers around the agricultural year. Seed time and harvest festivals are presided over by a tribal chief who is believed to be some great tribal ancestor who is reincarnated.

Inside this official religion, and tolerated by it, is an esoteric cult confined to a sect of magicians. It is embodied in a secret society to which only men can belong. The members are all hunters, for sport not necessity, as is the case with the Dogon generally.

Like the *vinyau* secret society that hid their costumes in a rock shelter on Chenchere Hill, north of Dedza in Malawi, the Dogon hunting cult, known as "The Masks," repair to their shelter, which is, of course, taboo to anyone else, and make their masks there. The masks, usually depicting an animal's head, are then worn at secret dances. Attached to the masks are skirts of red fibers, similar to the split reed costumes of the vinyau, in which the initiated believe their magic power to reside. So as to ensure that all this magic does not backfire on its owner, the wearer of the mask is careful to draw a picture of the mask that he will wear on the wall of a rock shelter before he puts it on for the first time. If they did not do this, the initiated believe, the spirits of the animals that they have killed since the last time they danced in a mask would now harm them.

The society is not wholly religious. Just as elsewhere in Africa, religious power is associated with political power as well. The rulers of the Dogon state are practically all drawn from the members of the society. The chief is so much concerned with the ceremonies necessary to ensure a good harvest that he leaves most of the decisions to them, and by a convenient myth the tribal ancestor whom he reincarnates is considered to be the father of the founder of the Mask Society.

It is tempting to see in this artistic, religious, and political grouping the solution of many of our problems with regard to rock painting. Francis Klingender[7] has suggested that we have many lessons to learn from the painters of Dogon and this is no doubt true. Obstacles in transferring the situation in Dogon into the context of what we know about the rock painters are very great, however. The Dogons have reached quite a high rung on the ladder of civilization and have a secure life based on agriculture. Dressing up and wearing disguises is not unique to them — it goes on in all civilized societies. What we need to find, and what we have not found is a society of herdsmen and hunters who carry out ceremonial paintings. No such society exists nowadays and possibly none such ever did exist — except for the hunter artists of a Africa. It is this unique situation that gives African rock art its special quality.

[7]Klingender, *Animals in Art and Thought*, p. 23.

6

The People of the Paintings

Who were the artists of the rock? Opinion has always been divided on this subject and probably always will be. All I can do is to suggest some of the arguments that have been put forward, on one side or another, and then try to draw some sort of conclusion from the argument.

The arguments for a Bushman, or at least a Bushmanoid origin and continuance of the art have always been considerable. For a long time, as I have already noticed, no one dreamt of finding any other authors for the paintings than the Bushmen.

"The celebrated Bosjeman paintings," wrote J.G. Wood in 1871, "are scattered through the country, mostly in caves and on rocks near water springs . . . (they) . . . are often as well drawn as those produced so plentifully by the American Indians. They almost invariably represent figures of men and beasts, and in many cases the drawing is sufficiently good, to enable the spectator to identify the particular animals which the native artist had intended to delineate."[1]

The Bushman was not merely the painter in residence. He was the African troglodyte. All the other inhabitants of South Africa merely lived in caves intermittently. The Bushman did have other homes, "nests" in the trees, lean-to shelters, even excavated holes in the ground, but the size of some of

[1] Wood, *The Natural History of Man*, p. 297.

the middens outside his cliffside dwellings indicated that he had lived in them, off and on, for a long time. The Bushman was also the person whose way of life squared best with that of the people portrayed in the pictures. He was a simple hunter whose whole way of life centered around animals, such as those portrayed in the paintings. He did not build himself permanent houses like the Bantu, houses that were then beautifully decorated with wall paintings. Apart from the parietal art, which early visitors could see in Bantu huts, and which Bantu mineworkers were still painting in their homes as late as 1939 in the Rhodesian mining areas, *no one had ever seen any African race making any paintings at all.* It looked as though the painters had to be the Bushmen because there were no other candidates. Moreover what was known about Bushman technical painting methods, such as mixing fat with paint, fitted the old paintings, which often had a "halo" of fat, and otherwise approximated very much in colors, style, and subjects those paintings which Baines and other white men had seen the Bushmen making.

Those members of the vanishing race who were questioned about their arts had answers that, if not always wholly convincing, were at least all the answers that appeared to be forthcoming at all. When questioned about the paintings the average Bantu reaction was a shrug of the shoulders. They knew nothing about them, nor were they interested.

Why should the Hottentots have been regarded as possible rival painters? It is rather difficult to say why the idea first got around, though, as we have seen, various inquirers who had asked Bushmen about the paintings had gotten very indifferent answers. The Hottentots were very like the Bushmen. Before they had adopted white habits they must have been a hunting and a herding folk rather like the tall people in the battle and hunting paintings. Herds of cattle, flocks of long-tailed sheep, which appeared in many southwest Cape pictures, seemed to suggest the Hottentots much more than the Bushmen.

There was a good deal of evidence that the painters had mingled and mixed with many foreigners, who were figured in the paintings. Whether these strangers were Herero or Bergdama horn blowers, Bantu warriors, or visitors whose provenance cannot be immediately ascertained, like the White Lady, but who have a very far away look about them, it was much more likely that the Hottentots would be in touch with them rather than the Bushmen, who seem to have been a shy people who dreaded contacts with foreigners, contacts in which they always came off the worse.

Primitive as the Bushman way of life was, it could not have been carried on in Africa for an indefinite period, certainly not as far back as some of the paintings now proved to date from. Paintings were discovered, covered by stalactic layers of cave deposits, flaked from cave walls and buried by occupation layers, and supplied with an impeccable pedigree of age by radio carbon dating, chromatographic analysis of pigments, and sequential relation to other dated paintings or to occupation layers either of human debris, or, in the Sahara to guano deposits or cattle bones.

The trend of research has been to throw back the dates of rock paintings further and further. Those from the Sahara were once estimated to be as old as 5,000 years, those from the Horn of Africa 4,000, Kenyan paintings were taken to be 1,500 years old, Zambian 6,300 years old, Rhodesian 7,000 years old and South African 6,000 years old.[2]

Now, however, on the basis of the occupation layers associated with cave paintings, the Rudners have argued that the Rhodesian engravings may be 7450 B.C., while Zambian art may date from 5590 B.C. and Tanzanian from 4360 B.C.

[2]Cooke, *Rock Art of Southern Africa*, p. 146.

The extension of the date of the paintings so far back worried scholars like Willcox, who had at first been prepared to see in the rock art schools a mere projection backwards in time of the work of the historic Bushmen.

The real problem lay in tacking modern races such as the Bushmen and the Hottentots onto the early men who must have been ultimately responsible for the beginnings of the art.

Likely early candidates now began to emerge in the Wilton Men. While one wave of the Wilton hunters built up the art of painting and developed it to great heights in South Africa, southwest Africa and Rhodesia, it was argued, new waves of Wilton people, not merely hunters but shepherds as well, took the same path as their predecessors, from Zambia, Rhodesia, and Botswana, to southwest Africa. Some groups of the Wilton People, it was felt, may have added cattle to their way of life and emerged as Hottentots.

In the eastern regions of South Africa Wilton shepherds came into contact with the Bushmen, who were representative of another type of early man, the Smithfield. The two ways of life became fused, and the synthetical group of people thus evolved created the supreme paintings of the Drakensberg.

So much for South Africa and central Africa, but what about the remainder of the continent? Obviously diffusion must have taken place, but for what reason and in which direction? Who had created the great schools, among others of Tassili, and Ain Dona in the El Awenat plateau?

The fact that European prehistorical art was so much older than African rock art, together with the remarkable resemblance between Eastern Spain, North Africa, the Sahara, Egypt, and the center and south, had made many argue that at some far distant time artists who were both hunters and herdsmen had roved from the Mediterranean to the Cape, wandering over a yet green and fertile Sahara to the open plains of East Africa and trekking down the tsetse-free corridors that run from north and south. They had moved across the savannahs with an eye to good hunting country, stopping at the mountainous plateaux that stood in their way and in which most of the paintings have been found but avoiding the very high mountains and the immense forests, such as those of the Congo.

The hunter artists, though no doubt racially mixed, must have enjoyed the coherence of a common way of life, a common religion, and certainly a culture so

Lion hunt at Glengyle. (Painting by Helen Tongue. Photo by Stella Mayes Reed.)

homogeneous that it is possible to try to interpret Eastern Spanish paintings in the light of Rhodesian frescoes. Different regional schools had evolved in consequence of the vast distances involved, but on the whole homogenity had been more remarkable than diversity.

The cultural trail seemed clearly marked; in Spain aniconic men brandished bows and arrows in monochrome paintings in the same sort of shelter that could have contained paintings in North Africa. In Algeria, almost identical paintings were to be found, while around the painted caves were scattered flint tools belonging to a small flake technique called the Capsian. Southward the trail ran clear. Perhaps the Capsians had been Europeans — the men of Tassili appeared to contain both white and negroid groups side by side — which was not an unusual occurrence in Africa. Part of the force of the Tassili civilization had gone off in the direction of Egypt, where echoes of the Sahara were to be found in weapons, dress, and even the stance of the frescoed figures. Another part of Tassilian civilization, after absorbing various influences from the Mediterranean, was deflected southward.

The farther away from the Sahara that art moved, the less its resemblance to Tassili grew to be, but isolated figures such as the White Lady served to recall the Saharan school, even at a very great distance.

Not all scholars were agreed that this had been the march of diffusion. Burkitt and Breuil argued that the art must be the movement of people, not ideas. It was not the styles of painting that had moved, but the painters themselves, either from Spain to Africa, or the other way round. African invasions of Spain, or

Spanish invasions of Africa, were both equally probable in the light of later Mediterranean history, but this thesis did not satisfy Alexander R. Willcox, who argued[3] that somewhere in the Sahara was the center of a Bushman cultural diffusion, from which influences had radiated north, to Tassili, northeast to Spain, southward to central and southern Africa and eastward to Egypt. Thereafter, the Bushmen painters, hounded by the advancing Bantu, had retreated further southward, till the upper millstone of the black race met on the lower of the white and crushed them.

Into this diversity of diffusionist theories the Rudners have thrown their own bombshell. They dismiss the suggestion that the Paleolithic art of Spain was imported into Africa, go on to scout the idea that rock art arose in comparatively late, Neolithic times, and instead point to the array of impressively early dates for central and southern African painting sites, such as 10,000 B.C. for Ohrigstad in the Eastern Transvaal.[4]

In view of these early dates, they argue, rock painting must have originated in South Africa and moved northward, where the dates for the painted sites are much later, those in the Sahara, for example, having been produced between 3500 and 2500 B.C.

Rock painting was no isolated phenomenon, say the Rudners. It was associated with improved flint knapping, which produced the small flake (microlith) blades. These were used in the bow and arrow, which had been invented in South Africa, and the use of this new weapon made hunting so much more efficient that a hunter now no longer had to spend his whole week hunting. It was enough to go out twice, perhaps once a week, and the resulting leisure was canalized toward the production of rock art.

While postulating the South African origin of rock art and its subsequent spread northward to East Africa and thence to North Africa the Rudners do not discount the possibility that it may have been fertilized and regenerated by the arrival of Neolithic influences from the Near East. Prominent among groups who might have contributed to such a cultural infusion are the Nachikufuans, a mixed, Caucasoid, Bushmanoid, and Negroid race, supposedly immigrants from Asia, who had invaded Zambia and whose influence can be felt in Rhodesia.

[3] Quoted in A.R. Willcox, *Drakensberg*, p. 24.

[4] J. and I. Rudner, *The Hunter and His Art*, p. 220ff.

127

It is in the light of this preliminary discussion that we must now approach the people of the paintings. It would be as well to remember that it is difficult to stick national labels onto any art or any artist. All good art is international and by creating it the artist becomes an internationalist. It is very easy to make wrong attributions even today. If we visit a gallery and the display is of paintings by an artist with a Polish name, and we see someone standing talking to the gallery director, someone who wears turned up moustaches with waxed ends, like a Polish gentleman of the old school, we might then take a risk, go up to him and say: "I like your paintings." But how many chances there are of being wrong in a guessing game of this sort!

It is far safer to regard the galleries of Africa as being the work of a mixed body of painters. Like any other art gallery, they contain the work of more than one national school, and many regional schools. The men of Wilton and Nachikufu have contributed. Bushamanoids, Negroids, and Caucasoids have all played their part in the early stages, giving what they had to the paintings. At the end of the day Bushmen continued to paint to the last, Negroes added tentative imitations to the earlier masterpieces, and Caucasians indelibly stamped the art with their impress by copying many of the works that are now lost. It was a truly composite picture, painted by a committee of mankind. It is almost impossible to sort out the attributions and most of what we know rests on conjecture. Wilton and Nachikufu men are assumed to have painted the caves in which they lived. I certainly do not intend to paint my house if I can get an outside specialist to do the job. We know that the Bushmen were considered such good arrow makers that other tribes bought arrows from them by bartering game. It is not beyond the bounds of conjecture that the Nachikufuans and the Wiltons employed outside painters, though it is of course, very unlikely.

The Stone Age folk who certainly were inhabitants of the caves that they painted were the men of Tassili. The first European expatriate had arrived in Africa around 50,000 B.C. in the person of Neanderthal Man. Forty thousand years later came a fresh wave of immigrants, the Cro-Magnons, representatives of a people who in Europe had been associated with a vigorous school of cave painting. It is no accident that North Africa, too, now began to develop a rock art school.

The Cro-Magnons succeeded in establishing themselves in the western part of North Africa, while the eastern high plateaus of the Constantine area, with what is now Tunisia, remained the province of a mysterious race called Rammadyates, who lived mainly on snails. Various other neolithic types of life began to emerge in North Africa, with a particular interest, the Capsians who had the same kind of small flake weapons as the prehistoric painters of Eastern Spain.

The Tassilians are the most academic of all prehistoric painters, and it is possible to deduce a lot more about them than about any other prehistoric folk. They went naked or wore a small loin cloth, but they had developed a kind of headgear that recalls that of ancient Egypt. Their skin color varied from white, as in the famous aniconic girl at Tin Teferiet, to a dark red brown, but there is no certainty that here, or anywhere else, realistic colors were used to portray skin. Women, it has been suggested, were plumper in pictures than they really were, and they were painted with swaying hips, often accompanied by lordosis, because this was the accepted norm of good looks for women at the time. Men, the ultimate judges of what constitutes feminine good looks, certainly preferred fat women in parts of the Mediterranean and North African area at this time. Enormously plump goddesses appear in Malta, while among the Berber communities, with whom the Tassilians may be associated, women were actually fattened by being force fed by a funnel.

The Peuls of North Africa, a dark-skinned race, the copper-colored and long-haired Fulani, and the white Berbers have all been suggested as possible descendants of the men of Tassili.

What is so striking about the Tassili paintings is that for a time at least they lift the veil on the human face. Portraits appear that some have seen as animal masks. Although the faces of the subjects are fringed with hair (which may be a false beard in the Egyptian style) I feel that I can recognize the simian characteristics of the Bushmen in these paintings.

Like the Hottentots the Tassilians lived on the milk of the innumerable cows that they kept, and they even had a surplus of milk that they used for painting — casein has been found used as a fixative in the paints. Possibly milk was sacred to them as it was in the Hottentot society, and jars of milk appear to figure as sacrifices. They also lived on the game run down by their hounds or killed by their throwing sticks and arrows. Because the climate was so much more humid than it is now in the Sahara when the

"Filiform Men," from a Rhodesian cave. *Photo courtesy of the Rhodesian Information Service.*

Giraffe and hunters, Rhodesia. *Photo courtesy of the Rhodesian Information Service.*

Paintings in Mrewa Cave, Rhodesia. *Photo Mrs. S. A. Bunyan.*

Part of the Drakensberg Range, where the Bushmen made their last stand. *Photo courtesy of the South African Tourist Corporation.*

A Hottentot in European dress. *Photo by Stella Mayes Reed.*

first paintings were made, game must have abounded near to the caves, which have been scoured out by spates of the streams that once ran through the *oueds*. Though the Tassilians painted the caves, they do not seem to have lived in them permanently. They may have been places of refuge during the wet season, when the huts made of straw or branches that they lived in at other times must have become very uncomfortable. The abundance of wild grains that they collected and ground between millstones and grinders also testify to how damp the climate must have been then.

Like all the other rock painters whose work we shall examine the Tassilians seem to have had a very disturbed history, in its later stages at least. The peaceful pastoral life they had enjoyed was shattered by the arrival of invaders from Crete and other parts of the Aegean, "people of the sea" who rode in chariots, and whose art is apparently reflected in the "flying gallop," a Cretan art convention that appears in some of the paintings.

Much later, other figures appear riding camels, figures who are probably enemies, for in the desert, an oasis such as Tassili was a coveted prize that would in the end go to the strongest and most determined adversary. The mere appearance of the camel indicates how far dessication had progressed, and the Tassilians were probably only saved from complete enslavement by the camel-riding nomads by the drying up of the water supplies, which drove everyone from the area. Only prolonged excavations will tell us what really happened at Tassili.

The mantle of rock painting now descends on the shoulders of Nachikufu Man, who appears around 3940 B.C., in time to receive the spark of inspiration from the Tassilians, whom in some ways he resembled. Though rather a shadowy figure, he is known to have possessed Bushman, Caucasoid, and Negroid traits.

The Nachikufuans, who are supposed to have orginated rock painting in East Africa, were strong in Zambia, where the rock shelter of Nachikufu, thirty miles south of Mpika, in the Muchinga Hills, the type shelter of the culture, showed that the inhabitants made small flakes ("microliths") that were presumably used for tipping arrows. The Nachikufuans, who had fled before the Bantu arrived or been exterminated by them, were presumed to have painted the cave with the realistic pictures still to be found in it, and a rock shelter nearby, with schematic not realistic frescoes.

Among the other remains of the Nachikufuans discovered in the cave were ochre crayons, grindstones, pestles, and lumps of pigment. As in all discoveries of this sort, it is a mere assumption that these paints were used for painting the shelter they could equally well have been used for body paint, which was at least as important as cave painting in old Africa. Along with the painting equipment were found polished axe heads, scrapers, and bored stones, such as those which would weigh down a digging stick, like those used by later Hottentots and Bushmen.

Wilton Man was a Central and South African cousin of East African Nachikufuan Man. Preceded by a forebear called Pomongwe Man, also a painter, the Wiltons appear some time around 5660 B.C. Much more diversified than the Nachikufuans as regards getting a living, the Wiltons lived in open sites, rock shelters, and by shell mounds on lake shores. This latter trait is particularly interesting when taken in conjunction with the fact that the teeth of a number of elderly folk whose skeletons have been found are unworn, presumably because they lived on a diet of shellfish which, like modern oysters, could be swallowed whole. Other Wiltons were much more concerned with hunting; they lived surrounded by an abundance of half-moon-shaped scrapers, which, like the later Bushmen, they probably used to shape their bows and arrows, and also to scrape and dress the skins that they turned into karosses or leather bags. They may also have used the scrapers to strike fire from iron pyrites lumps. They made coarse pottery, some of it burnished.

After death, Wiltons were laid in shallow graves in the crouched-up position in which Hottentots slept, and in which Hottentots, too, were buried, wrapped up in a worn out kaross.

The Wilton race are often spoken of as being the fathers both of the Hottentots and the Bushmen — with Smithfield Man as the immediate founding father of the Bushman people. Racially, the Wiltons had pronounced Bushman traits, with a round head, arched forehead, poorly developed brow ridge, massive mandibles, and a jutting out chin. He had a thick skull, and was apparently massively built. Not all these traits sound either Bushmanoid, or Hottentot, suggesting that ethnographically speaking, it is a wise child that knows his own father.

Descendants of the Wiltons, the Saan Bushmen, and the Bergdama, a mysterious black race that may have come from North Africa via the Sudan, were still painting in Bergdama and around the Drakensberg in the late nineteenth century. They had been enslaved by the Saan Bushmen and the Hereros, an indication that the Bushmen were just as ready to enslave another folk as their neighbors were to enslave them.

Though much more like one another than any other race, the Hottentots and the Bushmen were so different from one another that they have had very opposed destinies. The Hottentots were the industrious apprentices of the Wilton Race, the Bushmen the idle ones. To put it in a different way, the Hottentots succeeded in meeting and assimilating modern civilization; they have become absorbed in the class known in South Africa as the "Cape Coloreds." The Bushmen did not even try to adopt the new ways brought by the white men. Apart from a remnant left in the Kalahari, some of whom are now trying to gear themselves to modern ways by becoming house boys, they have died out or been exterminated.

The Hottentots seem to have had as little time for their close relatives, the Bushmen, as anyone else. They must have ousted them from many parts of their original range, though it is difficult to be sure about this, because we do not know just how much territory was occupied originally by the Hottentots. In historical times, they were confined to South Africa.

Physically, the Hottentot stood a few inches taller than the Bushman, but marriage between the two races has brought them nearer together as regards size. The Hottentots had small hands and feet. They carved wooden milk jars, called *bambus.* "A European," says Wood,[5] "would not be able to make the smaller sizes of these jars, as he would not be able to pass his hand into the interior. The hand of the Hottentot is however, so small and delicate that he finds no difficulty in the task." The small size of the hands and feet of both Hottentots and Bushmen is important because Alexander R. Willcox has suggested that the palm print paintings are too small to be those of anyone other than the Bushmen.

The Hottentot had an apricot-colored skin, a profile like that of the Bushman, hair that was arranged in "peppercorns" on the head, and his womenfolk showed the traits of steatopygia, and elongation of the *labia minora.* Francis Galton, the Victorian explorer and ethnographer, described his astonishment at the development shown by Mrs. Petrus: "the lady who ranks second among all the Hottentots for the beautiful outline that her back affords."[6] "I profess to be a scientific man," Galton continues, "and was exceedingly anxious to obtain accurate measurement of her shape, but there was a difficulty in doing this. I did not know a word of Hottentot and could never, therefore explain to the lady what the object of my foot rule could be; and I really dared not ask my worthy missionary host to interpret for me. I therefore felt in a dilemma as I gazed at her form, that gift of bounteous nature to this favored race, which no mantua maker, with all her crinoline and stuffing can do otherwise than humbly imitate.

"The object of my admiration stood under a tree, and was turning herself about to all points of the compass, as ladies who wish to be admired usually do. Of a sudden my eye fell upon my sextant; the bright thought struck me and I took a series of observations upon her figure in every direction, up and down, crossways, diagonally, and so forth, and I registered them carefully upon an outline for fear of any mistake. This being done, I boldly pulled out my measuring tape, and measured the distance from where I was to the place she stood, and having thus obtained both base and angles, I worked out the result by trigonometry and logarithms.[7] The elongation of the *nymphae* or *labia minora* which are sometimes called a 'Hottentot apron,' and which are described as being in the Bushwomen, like the wattles of a turkey cock, were another very unusual Hottentot trait, and one would have expected to find some expression of this characteristic in one of the rock paintings."

Bruzen de la Martiniere, the Spanish Geographer Royal, talking about the Hottentots, remarks that they frequently amputated one testicle when they were young, "claiming that this helps greatly to preserve and augment their agility."[8] Another early writer about the Bushmen says that they push their testicles into the loose skin of the scrotum at the base of the penis when they are going to indulge in any active pursuit. It is this trait, I feel, that can be observed, in a petrograph that Willcox reproduces showing a man with a virile member without any testicles showing, and not semicastration.

[6]Ibid., p. 243.

[7]Ibid.

[8]Bruzen de la Martiniere, *Le Grand Dictionnaire Géographique, Historique Et Critique,* (Paris: Les Libraires Associés 1768), 3:40.

[5]Wood, *The Natural History of Man,* p. 252.

It is almost impossible to believe everything that one reads about the characteristics of the Hottentot and Bushmen races. Did the Bushgirl who seduced W. Harris's guard, who had been placed to keep watch on his cattle, so that her relatives were able to steal some and kill the rest, *really* have a footmark that was only four inches long? Harris assures us that she did, and since he tracked the girl and her relatives along their escape route, he may be correct.

Early Hottentots wore a very slight girdle, a kaross, and a cap that covered their scanty hair. Sometimes, they would make their cap by rubbing their heads with clay. These applied caps, ornamented with feathers and other finery, may account for some of the strange headdresses to be seen in the pictures. Hottentots also rubbed their bodies with cosmetics that included grease, a mineral powder called *sibilo*, which had a steel grey or bluish luster and was probably specular iron, and *buchu,* a vegetable powder made from fragrant croton and other plants. The naked, red painted figures of the rock pictures would, then, look not unlike an early Hottentot.

The Hottentots were fond of wearing ostrich shell beads — an ornament that turns up in many excavated cave sites. These beads, says Wood, were "made by laboriously cutting ostrich shells into thin circular discs, varying in size from the sixth of an inch to nearly half an inch in diameter and pierced through the middle. Many hundreds of these discs are closely strung together, so as to form a sort of circular rope, white as if made of ivory. Sometimes this rope is long enough to pass several times round the body, against which the shining white discs produced a very good effect." Either beads of this sort or body paint account for the white spots in lines that ornament so many figures in the paintings. Needless to say, when the white spots appear on hair, as they do in the *White Lady of the Brandberg,* they can only be ostrich shell beads.

The Hottentots were expert hide curers. From the skins of their oxen, they made karosses, skin garments with the hair outside, with which they covered themselves and in which they were buried. Hide garments and hide rugs have been seen in many of the paintings, particularly those which depict burial rites. The Hottentots also made hide ropes, as well as acacia bark ropes. Ropes are seen in many paintings where men are carrying bundles that have obviously been lashed together. Skin bags, which also figure in the paintings, were also made very ingeniously by the Hottentots. They were formed from two layers of skin, the inner with the hair inward, the outer with the flesh side out. Loads carried in bags of this sort would travel absolutely unspoiled even by the most torrential rain.

The Hottentots carried weapons that were virtually indistinguishable from those of the Bushmen. They consisted of bows and arrows, a single assegai (adopted from the Bantu), and knobkerries and throwing sticks. The Hottentot was a deadly shot with the throwing stick, which accounted for the "rats and mice and such small deer," on which these strange folk were content to live when they were not able to obtain milk products or big game.

Though primarily a herdsmen, the Hottentot was an occasional hunter. He killed game by his arrows or by driving it over ravines, into pitfalls, or up to massed bowmen in ambush. Strandlopers, beach-combing Hottentots who lived on shellfish as well as on the occasional stranded whale, and pastoral

Lion chasing a man and other strange figures, one of which may be a food root. Advance Post. (Painting by Helen Tongue. Photo by Stella Mayes Reed.)

131

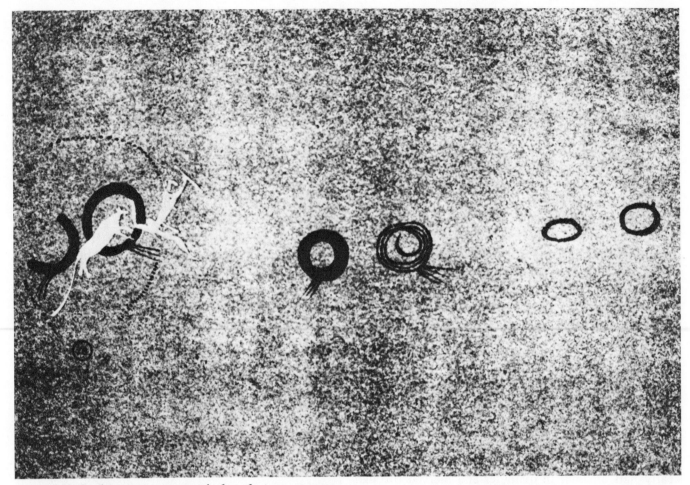

Leopard chasing men across circles that may represent pits or pools. (Painting by Helen Tongue. Photo by Stella Mayes Reed.)

Hottentots alike gorged themselves whenever there was an opportunity to eat large quantities of meat. In the climate of South Africa, as Wood points out, gluttony was all the more excusable in that the meat would not keep for long, though neither Hottentots nor Bushmen would have turned up their nose at a piece of game that was too "high."

The gargantuan meals that occurred on occasions of this sort intoxicated the Hottentots, and the excited poses in which the painters have placed some figures that stand around slaughtered animals may owe their origin to this circumstance.

A more usual diet for the Hottentot was milk, which he ate from a bowl with a spoon made from the stem of a fibrous plant called *umphombo*. The stem, which was flattish and about an inch in width, was cut into suitable lengths and soaked in water. It was then beaten between two stones until the fibers separated from one another. Such a brush-spoon, used to convey liquid to the mouth, could equally well have been used to brush paint onto a cave wall.

One of the reasons for the enmity between Bushmen and Hottentots was that the former were always raiding the cattle of the latter. The Hottentots were great herdsmen and shepherds, and the flocks of sheep and cattle that appear in the paintings are a clue to their creators. The Hottentots were always moving in search of pasture, and on the move they lived in kraals of huts made from branches and covered with skins and matting that the Hottentot women could erect and strike in a matter of minutes. These kraals were guarded by specially trained oxen, like watchdogs, who would admit no strangers. Other cattle were kept as pets. The Hottentots had a wonderful eye for a cow or ox. If he saw an animal, just once, even at night, he would remember it and recognize it after a lapse of years. Cattle played a very important part in their lives and entered into their religion as well, just as they did into that of the men of Tassili.

"When they need rain for their pastures," says

Moreri, "they ask for it from a certain Being whom they do not know, whom they do not name, and who lives, so they say, high, and they offer him a sacrifice of milk, which is the best thing that they have."[9]

A happy-go-lucky people, the Hottentots were fond of dancing and singing. There were dances for men and women together, and all-women dances such as the melon dance. Some of the postures of the painted figures are almost certainly those of dancers. They played a game that they called "card playing," though Wood was puzzled by the name, since no cards were used. It was rather like Morro, a game that is played in southern Europe, and it consisted in hiding a piece of stick in one hand, and then throwing out both hands closed to an opponent, who was invited to guess which hand held the stick. Again, this game may be figured in some of the paintings.

Massage may also explain some of the unusual postures of some painted figures. "The patient lies prostrate," says Wood, "while a couple of women, one on either side, pound and knead him with their closed fists, at the same time uttering loud cries close to his ear."

Peaceful shepherds living in a very loosely organized society in which authority was confined to the headmen of the village, the Hottentots were no match for the well-organized, tall, brown-skinned warriors who began their trek south from east Africa about the tenth century. The Bantu (a term referring to the language spoken by the group, like Languedoc in France) moved southward by easy stages so as not to tire their herds of cattle, consolidate their conquests and incorporate the defeated as a subject race. The existence of the tsetse fly belt must have halted them while they explored for tsetse-free corridors. Their martial bearing, wonderful musculature (Bantu women can pick up and carry on their heads loads of wood that a white man could not even raise from the ground), their iron weapons, shields (a partial protection from the poisoned arrows of the Hottentots and Bushmen) assegais, and knobkerries must have struck terror into the hearts of the Hottentots. Pictures of the Bantu, on many rock walls, testify to the effect they had on the light-skinned races that they now proceeded to colonize.

There was no employing a Bushman to do anything. He refused to work except for himself, so he was quickly exterminated by the Bantu wherever they arrived. The Hottentots were more adaptable.

[9]Louis Moreri, *Le Grand Dictionnaire Historique* (Paris: Jean Baptiste Coignard, 1725), 4:671.

They were content to live as a subject race, and it now began to dawn on them that they might have a choice of being subject either to the Bantu or the whites.

White South Africans had begun to arrive at the Cape from the seventeenth century onward. They had found the Hottentots very useful as farm labor, while the Hottentots themselves were quick to adopt white ways. The white settlers were called "Boers," a name that means "countryman" in Holland, where most of them came from. There were some French Huguenots in their midst, but these very soon became completely assimilated to colonial Dutch ways. After the capture of the Cape from Napoleon by the British lots of English settlers came to farm there, some of them ex-officers who had been given land grants.

It was British policy to keep white settlers from clashing with the indigenous folk in the colonies and

Figures dancing, hunting, and holding a bow, which may be a musical one. (Painting by Helen Tongue. Photo by Stella Mayes Reed.)

This Hottentot Kraal illustrates a more permanent encampment. Many kraals have been suggested to occur in the paintings, particularly the schematic ones. From Wood. (Photo by Stella Mayes Reed.)

to prevent the oppression of the natives so far as it was possible. This policy had led to the War of American Independence, because George III regarded the land west of the Alleghenies as a permanent reserve for the Indians and the colonists had other ideas. The policy was also going to lead to a whole series of wars in South Africa, in which the British either fought the Boers or moved in to repress the advancing Bantu.

Around 1815, a Bantu king called Chaka had united one group of the Bantu called the Zulu. He had been impressed by British military discipline by watching soldiers drilling, and had decided he, too, wanted a discliplined, highly trained army. Though the Zulus afterward acquired rifles, their primary arm always remained the assegai, which Chaka shortened and taught them to use as a sort of bayonet, a short, stabbing spear that could only be used at close quarters instead of being flung from a distance, like the old assegai.

Armed with the new weapon led by Chaka's military genius, stiffened by a discipline so severe that nothing like it has ever been seen before or since, Zulu influence spread over south and central Africa, apparently irresistibly. Zulu generals knew there was no hope for an unsuccessful commander in the Zulu state, so rather than return without having achieved their mission and face death with fearful tortures they hastened to escape as far from Zululand as they

Sheep, oxen, and herdsman, who must be Bantu. (Painting by Helen Tongue. Photo by Stella Mayes Reed.)

could and found new kingdoms for themselves. Whole peoples, either exterminated, or set in motion by what Africans called the *mfecane* or "time of breaking," now began to spread confusion throughout the continent.

In this struggle the Hottentot realized that they had only one ally, the white settler. If they did not throw in their lot with the whites they too would soon become extinct, as the Bushman obviously would. What was more they felt the bitterest hatred for their Bantu conquerors.

The whites were quick to sense this antagonism and they employed the Hottentots as mercenaries and cattleguards. They could detect the presence of a Bantu cattle stealer (cattle stealing was considered very creditable among the Bantu as it was at one time in the Scottish Highlands). "Even on a dark night," says Wood, "when the dusky body of the robber can hardly be seen he will discover the thief, work his stealthy way towards him, and kill him noiselessly with a single blow."[10]

In the process of becoming an ally of the whites the Hottentot soon became culturally and to some extent racially lost in their midst. Before many years had elapsed it was hopeless to look to him for any explanation of the mysteries of rock art.

Unlike the Hottentot, the Bushman retained his way of life and primeval habits almost entirely. Many of his customs cannot have changed for centuries and they are reflected in the rock paintings. "The Bushmen," says Wood, "are a variety of the Hottentot race, which they closely resemble in many particulars. The peculiar form of the countenance, the high cheek bones, the little contracted eyes, and the long narrow chin, are all characteristics of the Hottentot race. The color of the skin, too, is not black, but yellow, and even paler than that of the Hottentot, and the women are notable for that peculiarity of form [steatopygia] which has already been noticed."[11]

The Hottentots and the Bushmen spoke an almost identical language, full of strange clicks, or as one Victorian traveler put it, "clicks and clacks." The Bushman, however, a born *improvisatore,* added to his spoken language many signs as well. "When a Bushman speaks," says Wood,[12] "he uses a profusion of gestures, animated, graphic, and so easily intel-ligible that a person who is wholly ignorant of the language can follow his meaning." Intelligible in conversation, these signs may be less intelligible when expressed in some of the rock paintings, as probably some of them are.

Though he loved to talk, no Bushman would willingly reveal his name in conversation. When a Bushboy took service with a settler he always assumed a Dutch name like Andries, Ruyter, Kleinboy, or Booy. This shyness about names undoubtedly arose from the belief that anyone who knew their names could use this knowledge to work magic against them. Probably for this reason, the faces of the figures in the cave paintings are disguised so that no one can recognize them.

Like the Hottentots, the Bushmen covered themselves with grease, *sibilo* and *buchu.* They wore a loin cloth and karosses or mantles made from animal skins, and because they had such tiny figures their whole bodies seemed to disappear in the folds of the kaross, like many figures in the paintings. Men rubbed their hair with grease and clay so thickly that the mixture became a kind of cap, in which they stuck

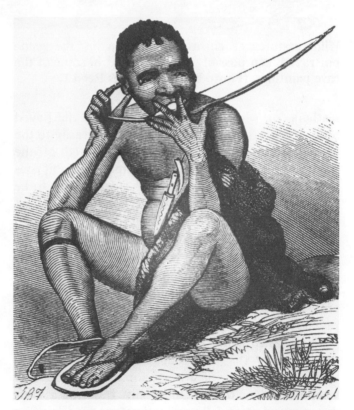

Bushmen playing the Goura, from William J. Burchell's *Travels in the Interior of Southern Africa,* London, 1824. Musical bows of this sort appear in several paintings. (Photo by Stella Mayes Reed.)

[10]Wood, *The Natural History of Man,* p. 240.

[11]Ibid.

[12]Ibid., p. 266.

Wild gestures, such as this shown in the game portrayed, can possibly be recognized in some of the cave paintings. (Photo by Stella Mayes Reed.)

feathers, or which they surmounted by the flayed head of some game trophy, which stuck easily to the cap. Whenever a Bushman killed a bird he cut off the head and fastened it to his head cap. This habit goes far to explain the many animal headed figures to be seen in the paintings.

When he was going to war or to the hunt, however, a Bushman's usual headdress was a crown of arrows stuck through his hair. Heads crowned with arrows can be seen in several of the paintings. The crown of arrows was partly intended for convenience — the arrows were there all ready to fire — and partly for psychological effect.

There was good reason for the enemy to be frightened by the sudden appearance of a Bushman, wearing his crown of arrows, for they were deadly weapons, and although they only flew for a short distance and were delivered with rather uncertain aim and vigor from the puny bow of the Bushmen, those whom they hit, or even grazed, died. I know of only one occasion when someone was struck by a Bush-

man arrow and escaped. A Dutch missionary was shot by a Bushman, but as luck had it, he had on his person a very thick tract. The arrow passed through the pages of the pamphlet, but by the time it entered his body, the poison had been rubbed off on the pages of the book and, to the great astonishment of everyone round about him, he did not die from the wound.

Hunters pure and simple, without cattle, or as someone put it, with "other peoples" cattle, the way of life of the Bushmen was dictated by the demands of the chase.

"A rock cavern," says Wood, "is a favorite house with the Bosjeman, who finds all the shelter he needs without being obliged to exert any labor in preparing it. But there are many parts of the country over which he roams in which there are no rocks and consequently no caves."[13]

Out in the veldt, far from mountains with caves in them, the Bushman selected a tree such as a mimosa or a tarconanthus, bent over its branches so as to form a tentlike covering, and lined it with soft

[13]Ibid., p. 274.

136

material such as hay, dried leaves, or wool. Such a treehouse looked like a giant bird's nest, and it was this habit of roosting in a tree that earned the Bushmen their name. They referred to themselves by a name that Wood transliterates as "Saqua." From the treehouse the Bushman could dart his poisoned arrow at any game that passed by.

Another Bushman home was made by scratching a hole in the ground, throwing up the earth to windward, and planting a few poles in the ground, over which a matting screen was thrown. If ever the Bushmen settled down to a permanent encampment, which was comparatively seldom, they formed a kraal by fixing flexible sticks in the ground, bending them over to assume a cagelike form, and covering them with simple mats made from reeds. A Bushman encampment of this sort looked much like a Hottentot one.

Many abstract paintings have been conjectured to represent either houses of this sort or, perhaps, whole kraals.

Many hunting methods that the Bushmen used have been found in the paintings, though not so many as were actually in use. I have, for example, looked in vain for an indisputable example of the ostrich-feather brooms used to make a fence to scare game into an ambush. The least disputable of these methods was that used in hunting ostrich, even though it is not confined to the Bushmen, as it was mentioned by Strabo in his description of Arabia.

The ostrich hunter made a very elaborate disguise for himself, consisting of a dressed ostrich skin with the feathers but without the legs, stretched over a framework that included a long pole to stiffen the neck and support the head. The framework rested on the Bushman's shoulders in such a way that it could

A Bushman encampment. Note the man with ostrich feathers in the foreground. The tree from which the poison for arrows was obtained appears in the background. From Wood. (Photo by Stella Mayes Reed.)

A slight hedge of reeds, such as those pictured in the paintings, constituted a house for Hottentots and Bushmen alike when there was nothing better available. From Wood. (Photo by Stella Mayes Reed.)

be thrown off at a moment's notice. The ostrich hunter rubbed his legs with white chalk, and was now ready for the chase.

Having spied a flock of ostriches from the rocky kopje on which he was keeping watch, he would don his framework and patiently creep upwind to the flock, approaching in a roundabout way and stopping every now and then to lower the head of the bird so as to give the impression it was feeding. Then, when he was close enough to a bird, he would drop the decoy skin, shoot any arrow into the bird, and don the skin again. The wounded ostrich would run away, followed by its companions and the disguised Bushman. Soon the poison would begin to take effect and as the ostrich fell to the ground its companions would gather round it commiseratingly, thus giving the hunter a chance to claim yet another victim.

Sometimes the ostriches would sense that there was something not quite right about the new member of the flock and gather round to attack it. This was a serious matter for the hunter – the beak or foot of an ostrich could easily deal a tiny fellow like him a mortal blow, so to avoid being pecked to death, he ran rapidly to windward of the flock, let them flair his scent, and thus panicked them.

As they stampeded he flung off his feather disguise and sent a volley of poisoned arrows into them till they were out of range. By another ingenious hunting method, Bushmen would bury themselves in the sand among the eggs of the huge ostrich nest, and shoot the best bird among the parents as they returned to their brood.

Ostrich shells were used by the Bushmen as water containers. They were sometimes engraved with line ornament that recalls that of the engravings or the paintings, and one of the most ingenious uses to which the Bushmen put them was to bury them, filled with water, along their line of retreat through some arid country across which they intended to drive stolen cattle.

138

Hunting rhinoceros with poisoned arrows. From the Charewa Cave, Rhodesia. (Photo Courtesy Rhodesian Ministry of Information.)

These caches of water, which were undetectable except to a Bushman, enabled the little people to cross the otherwise waterless desert, driving their spoils before them. Thirsty cattle that seemed on the point of death would be given a drink from a container. Meanwhile their pursuers, half dying of thirst, would give up and return back to their ravaged farms.

Because the hides of the elephants and rhinoceroses that the Bushmen hunted were too thick to be penetrated by an arrow, they arranged ingenious deadfalls and pits, or drove the great beasts over the edge of cliffs. Smaller animals were driven along the ostrich feather fences that I have mentioned.

The poisoned arrows of the Bushfolk have been mentioned more than once. They were envenomed with a very complicated toxin, which could take several forms. One was created by extracting the juices of some plants, such as some of the euphorbias, and combining it with venom from the glands of the puff adder or cobra. In order to collect cobra venom, the Bushman would creep up behind a cobra, put his foot on it, just behind the head so that it could not bite him, then attack its head with a stick so as to work it up to a pitch of fury before he finally killed it and extracted the poison. By following this procedure he believed that not merely would the poison glands be full of venom, but it would be venom of a particularly toxic quality. The poison thus obtained was boiled down in a pot made of hollowed-out sandstone until it assumed the color and consistency of pitch.

Another poison was made from a poisonous bulb, recognizable by its blue, undulating leaves that rose out of the ground to spread like a fan, while a third

139

The subject of this picture is the attack upon a rhinoceros by hunters armed with bows and arrows. This painting is located in the Charewa Elephant Cave, Rhodesia. (Photo Courtesy Rhodesian Tourist Board.)

was made from amaryllis juice, mixed with venom from a large black spider. These arrow poisons did not exhaust the armory of the Bushmen. They had a fourth, the most dreaded of all, because a victim wounded by it died in the most frightful agony, accompanied by madness, either caused by delirium or by some element in the toxin itself. As David Livingstone put it, a victim of this poison "cuts he himself, calls for his mother's breast, as if he were returned in idea to his childhood again, or flies from human habitations a raging maniac."[14]

The source of this terrible poison was a tiny grub

called N'gwa which lived on the branches of the *Maruru papurie* tree. The whole of the interior of the grub was deadly poison, and all that a Bushman had to do to poison the tips of his arrows was first to make sure he had no cuts or scratches on his finger-tips, then to gently squeeze the content's of the grub's abdomen over his arrowhead. Just in case he did poison himself by accident, he always kept the antidote handy. This was the root of a plant called *kala haetlwe,* chewed up and applied mixed with fat to the wound.

Quite possibly some of the animals who appear in the paintings prancing about may be writhing in the death agonies induced by this arrow poison. As for those which appear upside down, as not a few do, and waving their legs in the air, they may be suffering from having drunk the water from a poisoned water hole. This was another way the Bushmen had of obtaining food and it was one that made them very

[14]Ibid., p. 288.

unpopular, because, as will be seen from the following instance, they marked the poisoned water so that they knew of its danger, other people did not.

Moffat, Livingstone's father in law, who was on a visit to some Bushmen, drank by mistake from a pool of water that stood near the Bushman kraal, not realizing that a hedge of bushes round about the water was intended to be a warning notice. Then, "I began," he says, "to feel a violent turmoil within and a fullness of the system, as though the arteries would burst, while the pulsation was exceedingly quick, being accompanied by a slight giddiness in the head." Fortunately, Moffat's Bushmen hosts were at hand, and although they had no antidote to give him, they were able to assure him that he would recover once the crisis of the poisoning was past. They had been consternated at their friend's accident and were overjoyed at his survival.

The little people were by no means as bad as they were made out to be, but there were many who had a strong interest in blackening their characters, because they wanted to take their land, their women, and the game on which they existed. The Bushman's fault in their eyes was that he was not prepared to submit tamely to all the indignities and injuries heaped upon him, he was in fact like the animal in a French zoo whose label read:

"Cet animal est très méchant,
*Quand on l'attaque, il se defend."**

"Subjected, as they are," writes Wood, "to oppression on every side, and equally persecuted by the Kaffirs [another word for the Bantu, from the Arabic, meeting 'infidels'] and the white colonists, it is not to be supposed that they could be remarkable for the benevolence of their disposition or their kindly feelings toward the hostile people with whom they are surrounded; and whenever they find an opportunity for retaliation, it is but natural that they should take advantage of it. Small, few, and weak, they would have been long ago exterminated but for their one weapon, the poisoned arrow."[15]

I have already suggested one of the reasons for the extermination of the Bushmen, their propensity for cattle stealing. They would creep into a cattle pen, whether Bantu or white, get close enough to the watchman to kill him with a poisoned arrow, select the best animals, and drive them off toward some

waterless district, where their pursuers would find it difficult to follow them and where they had concealed a line of ostrich shells filled with water, buried just below the surface of the ground. For some reason, which can perhaps best be explained as a desire to sacrifice to their god, they killed or maimed all the other cattle by stabbing them with arrows. The explanation usually given for this senseless and wicked act was that they were trying to wreak vengeance on the oppressors who had driven off the game from their waterholes. This could have been true in the case of the whites, who were great hunters, but I do not feel that it was so true of the Bantu, who neither hunted so much nor killed so many animals as the settlers.

Whatever the reasons for this practice, the results were fatal to the Bushmen. "The needless destruction which they work among the cattle," says Wood, "which to a Hottentot or Kaffir are almost the breath of life, has exasperated both these people to such a degree that they will lay aside for a time their differences and unite in attacking the Bosjeman, who is equally hated by both." The Bantu would get together in large enough numbers to crush any resistance from the small bodies of Bushmen, who usually moved in groups of family size, and who had, as has been already noticed, no chiefs, or even witch doctors, to organize them. Forming a shield wall and covering themselves with their large cowhide shields as a protection against the arrows that they dreaded just a little less than their commanders, they would push the Bushmen back into the rock shelters, in which the little people would make a last stand, shooting bravely at their enemies while there were any of them left alive.

"In such cases," says Wood, "the overwhelming numbers of the assailants and the absolute necessity of the task which they have set themselves are sure to lead to ultimate success and neither men nor women are spared. The very young children are sometimes carried off and made to act as slaves, but, as a general rule, the Kaffirs look upon the Bosjemans much as if they were a set of venomous serpents and kill them all with as little compunction as they would feel in destroying a family of cobras or puff adders."

There was not much that white and black could agree about in old South Africa, but they held identical views about the Bushmen. "It was a great surprise," wrote a Royal Artillery officer, Captain Drayson, writing shortly before 1874, "to notice the effect on our Dutch sporting companions of the

*"This animal is very bad — when you attack it, it defends itself."
[15]Ibid., p. 289.

intimation of 'Bushmen near.' We were riding on an elevated spur of the Drakensberg near the Mooi River, when a Boer suddenly reined up his horse and exclaimed.

'Cess! Kek der spoor van verdammt Bosjeman!'

"Jumping off his horse he examined the ground and then said, 'A man it is; one naked foot, the other with a *velschoen.'* The whole party immediately became intensely excited and scattered in all directions like a pack of hounds in cover. Some galloped to the nearest ridge, others followed on the spoor, all in search of the Bushman.

" 'He has not long gone,' said one of my companions, 'be ready.'

" 'Ready for what?' I inquired.

" 'Ready to shoot the *schelm.'*

" 'Would you shoot him?' I asked.

" 'Just so as I would a snake.'

"And then my companion explained to me that he had not long since bought at a great price a valuable horse which he had taken to his farm. In three weeks the horse was stolen by Bushmen. He followed quickly, and the animal being fat, began to tire, so two Bushmen who were riding it jumped off, stabbed it with their arrows, and left it. The horse died that night.

"Many other similar tales were told, our informant winding up with these remarks.

"I have heard that every creature God makes is useful, and I think so too; but it is only useful in its place. A puff adder is useful where there are too many toads, or frogs; but when he comes into my house he is out of place, and I kill him. A Bushman near my farm is out of place and I shoot him; for if I let him alone he poisons my horses and cattle and very likely me too."

The time is about 1870, and the place the Drakensberg. Time and place are so pat that it is tempting to regard these fleeing tracks as those of the last Bushman painter. Somewhere just over the ridge, he is trying to outdistance his pursuers, running along in the loping Bushman trot, carrying his weapons, and perhaps the *goura,* a Bushman harp packed up in the antelope skin knapsack he carries slung from his shoulders.

Like so many of the great arts of history, rock painting has been found to be "out of place" for its setting and the last of its exponents the heritor of ten millenia of an artistic tradition, is about to vanish from history.

7
The Purpose of the Paintings

European observers who have approached rock painting have often been armed with two preconceptions. One was that, somehow, African rock art was merely a carbon copy of its European counterpart, that of the late Stone Age. This idea was not on the face of it an unreasonable one. The remains of Cro Magnon and Capsian Stone Age dwellers, types of people who were known to have lived in Europe, had been found in North Africa.

What was more there was an astonishing similarity between the paintings of the rock shelters of Africa and those of eastern Spain. There, painted figures, not dissimilar to those to be found in Rhodesia or the Sahara, had been discovered, paintings that were ten thousand or even twenty thousand years old.

The New Stone Age folk were engravers as well as painters, and engravings continued to be made in Scandinavia down to about 500 B.C. In fact, Scandinavian rock engravings, which show some of the earliest ships, practically join hands with the incised carvings and sculptures of the Bronze and Iron Ages. It is possible to point to even more marked similarities between the art of the two countries. The strange spirals and circles, dumbbells and sun symbols, which appear on rock sites such as Twyfelfontein, could be paralleled on engraved boulders found in the British Isles, and over most of Europe.

It is then, not surprising that investigators felt that if there was community in the choice of motifs between the two continents of Europe and Africa,

then there must have been community of motivation as well.

Scholars are no longer wholeheartedly agreed that all cave paintings in Europe were made for purposes of sympathetic magic, and even if they were, that was no reason why the same should hold good in Africa.

The belief in a sympathetic magic origin arose partly from the discovery, in the cave of Montespan in France, of a secret sanctuary that could only be reached by diving beneath an overhanging rock and swimming through a subterranean stream. In an obscure chamber of the cave reached by this very roundabout route, there still stands today a life-sized bear modeled out of clay, but without a head. Near the bear, when it was found, lay a bear's skull and no doubt the model had been covered with a bear's skin with the head attached.

Other clay statues of animals in the same cave had been broken up, possibly with clubs, while in a yet deeper chamber there was painted on the cave wall a herd of horses being chased toward a pitfall. The horses painted on the wall were pitted with the marks of missiles, while the floor was still marked by the footsteps of many adolescents who in Paleolithic times had probably taken part in an initiation dance there.

Other indications of European cave art spoke of a desire to promote fertility. Ivory fetishes of very plump women with extremely well developed breasts and hips were made, and no doubt carried about by

143

It is easy to read an interpretation of "hunting magic" as the motive for cave painting into this frieze from the Manemba Cave, Mtoko District, Rhodesia, in which hunters confront galloping game. (Photo Courtesy Rhodesian National Tourist Board.)

Stone Age folk. Another cave "goddess" stood naked holding a horn, the symbol of sexual potency. Paintings of gravid animals and of magicians garbed in animal masks whose sexual intent was unmistakable, appeared on the walls of the deep European caves.

Two beautifully modeled bisons, about to couple, were discovered at Tuc d'Adoubert in France. Weird figures, strangely masked and robed, flitted through some of the cave paintings. They were, observers felt, obviously the official magicians whose task it was to preside over the promotion of sympathetic magic, at rites that would mime the actions necessary to promote good hunting and the fertility of the women of the tribe.

The belief that by acting out what you wanted to happen you could make it happen has had a very long history in European life. As late as the seventeenth century Sir Kenelm Digby was still asserting that if you put some of his "Powder of Sympathy" on the weapon, not the wound, the wound would heal up.

Indeed one reason that European scholars accepted the hypothesis that cave paintings were essentially magical was because their society was still deeply imbued with magic. As a small boy in Scotland I was brought up always to break my egg shell, after I had eaten the egg, otherwise witches would use the eggshell as a boat.

The belief that European cave paintings are concerned with magic rests on a rather large assumption. All the "hunting magic" objects could have been connected with some kind of game. Eskimos still try to spear a dummy figure of a bear, or a fox's skull, which is tied to a skewer. This is a sheer pastime, but if no one had recorded this game being played, and one of the dummy bears with the "spear" still tied to it had been found, it would have immediately been put down to sympathetic magic. The female figures might, again, have been made for amusement rather than serious magical intent.

So conditioned were the first observers of African rock art to the whole idea of sympathetic magic, however, an idea widely spread by such best sellers as Sollas' *Ancient Hunters,* that they had no hesitation in applying it to their paintings.

As early as 1909, Henry Balfour, writing a preface

144

to the Bushman paintings copied by M. Helen Tongue, commented that "it seems likely that the figures of animals may in many instances at any rate, have had a magical significance, the purport of their effigies being to bring success in hunting through the medium of 'sympathetic' magic in some form. Some of the hunting scenes may possibly have had the same application, and have represented the preludes to events rather than their record. The frequency with which human figures are represented surmounted by animals' heads is worthy of remark. These designs may in some cases represent the performance of symbolic dances by means of which the animals to be hunted were brought under magic influence and control, rendering them an easier prey to the hunter."

The same belief has been echoed, in our own day, by an authority as eminent as Alexander R. Willcox, who with great ingenuity has suggested that, just as a European witch sought to secure the nail pairings of her victim to work her spells, so the Bushmen increased the magical power of their pictures by painting them in pigment bound with marrow.

What evidence is there that sympathetic magic played any part in the art of the rock painters? Engravings of spoor, an indispensible prerequisite to a successful hunt, are to be found abundantly over Africa. One engraving site, Metsing, in Botswana on the southeast edge of the Kalahari Desert, figures the spoor of lions, baboons, rhinos, hippopotamuses, and many others. There are innumerable paintings of animals, of hunts, of quarries such as Bush pigs that have been riddled with spears (like some of the animals painted in the European caves, which have been shot with arrows). Hunters dressed in ostrich skin disguises close in on flocks of ostriches, which are unaware of their fate. Wounded animals gush blood from where they have been struck by missiles or from their mouths.

There are also many examples of dead animals, some of which are shown upside down. I have suggested elsewhere that this upside down position need not have been assumed to emphasize that they are dead. It may represent the fact that they had died from drinking from a water hole or stream poisoned by the hunters — in which case, they certainly would roll hooves up in the air. Other animals are shown laid out and being cut up by the hunters. Pelts, another product of the successful hunt, appear in some paintings.

The suggestions of fertility magic appear much more strongly than they do in prehistoric Europe. Though scenes of couples making love occur at Tassili, most of the sexual interest appears to be concentrated on the male. His virile organ is shown ornamented with tassels, oversize, and in a state of high sexual excitement (which may have been due to the Bushman habit of pushing the testicles into the base of the scrotum before beginning protracted and difficult chase through rough country). Males appear whose members appear to have been perforated with a stick (an attachment that would have acted as a sort of anchor and brought up anyone very short if he had tried traveling, equipped in this way, through thick bush).

It is certainly possible to point to myriad traits of the rock painter and say, "These could be sympathetic magic." For example the bodies of the elands in the paintings are usually elongated. This could be, as some have suggested, that elands do look like that, seen from a distance, or it could indicate the sympathetic magician's desire to obtain more steaks from his eland.

Even the distribution of particular animals may be significant. The Rudners have recorded no fewer than 142 occurrences of painted cattle from the Drakensberg, that area where the Bushmen, most doughty of cattle thieves, made their last stand.[1] Nonetheless some doubt must creep in about the magical intent of the paintings. There are no statues of animals that have been clubbed, as at Montespan. There is no sign that any of the paintings have been shot at by arrows — though as the Rudners point out, they might have been struck by small magic arrows such as the Bushman use, which would leave no trace.

There are other difficulties about the sympathetic magic explanation. At least some of the creatures portrayed on the rock paintings are those which no one would want to conjure up. This applies particularly to pythons and other reptiles such as crocodiles. No doubt the ancient hunters, like the Bushmen, ate them, but I do not expect that they really wanted to summon up a large vicious animal such as a crocodile, which had a scaly hide that was impervious to poisoned arrows.

In fact it is not at all easy to explain all the paintings as sympathetic magic, and Stow and after him Dorothea Bleek, Alexander R. Willcox, and Francis Klingender here brought into play another argument that appeared unassailable, namely that all the unexplained paintings are inspired by Bushman mythology and folklore.

Mythological interpretations stem from George

---

[1] J. and I. Rudner, *The Hunter and His Art*, p. 210.

A snake and some baboons. (Painting by Helen Tongue. Photo by Stella Mayes Reed.)

William Stow. The self-taught Warwickshire amateur archaeologist was very keen to accept the explanations that his Bushmen helpers offered him on two counts. On the one hand, they did give an explanation, of a sort, as to what the pictures were about, and no one likes to feel he is absolutely baffled by an aesthetic problem. On the other hand, if the Bushmen *could* explain the pictures then that proved they painted them, and this was something that Stow was very keen to prove, for he was a firm believer that all the paintings of South Africa were the work of the Bushmen, and that they were all of fairly recent date.

Furthermore, on the practical side, where else could Stow turn for any kind of help, except to the Bushmen? Moreover the numbers of the little people were dwindling every day, soon there would be no one left who could even pretend to interpret a rock painting. This may have made Stow all the keener to seize at what interpreters still existed, and he was impelled, too, by his fondness for and trust in his Bushmen friends.

Bushman folklore was vast, as Alexander R. Will-

cox has rightly pointed out, in referring to the immensity of the notes compiled on it by Bleek and his sister-in-law, Miss Lloyd. Yet these notes must have represented the merest fraction of the original body of folk lore, as it had once existed in the oral traditions of the tribesmen.

In another part of this book I suggested that the Bushmen may have invented some of the folklore stories that they retailed to please their white friends, and I also said that no Bushman had produced a pictured iconography of folklore, in the way, for example that converted Indians explained some of their beliefs to Spanish missionaries in America. I should qualify these statements by pointing out that the Bushmen were obviously born *improvisatori*. They were expected to embroider on the stories they told. The account given by Gordon Cuming's Bushman servant Ruyter of how he was nearly eaten by a lion to Cuming's friends in London was reckoned to be a very amusing entertainment — and it certainly seems to have gone on for some time.

Two Bushmen did in fact draw pictures to illus-

146

trate their mythology, but since one of them was a child, and the other was not a trained artist, these are of little use to us for iconographical purposes.

Bushman folklore was so extensive it would not be difficult to point to any picture and say that it had a mythological purport. Even a picture of a chameleon need not represent the creature itself, but its use for magical purposes, since chameleons were buried alive in certain areas in order to bring rain.

The general lines of the little peoples' folklore was as follows. They believed that they had emerged from a great hole in the ground — a cave or rock shelter in fact, and that they had then been followed out by the animals. All the stars and planets were anthropomorphized. The planet Jupiter, for example, was a man who spat out his daughters, just as Minerva emerged from the head of Zeus. Willcox has very rightly pointed out that this myth can only refer to the

One of the few paintings to illustrate a mantis, here chasing children. Rain falling into a pool, frogs, and humans are shown. (Painting by Helen Tongue. Photo by Stella Mayes Reed.)

moons of Jupiter, which are periodically eclipsed by her. The fact that the Bushmen could see Jupiter's moons at all with the naked eye indicates how good their eyesight must have been.

Although worshipped as a god, the Moon herself did not play nearly so large a part in mythological legends as did a mischievous creature, half-insect, half-human, called Kaggen, the Mantis. The Mantis Man, whom some have claimed to have recognized in certain rock paintings that occur as far away from the home of the historical Bushmen as Rhodesia, had as his mate, Dassie, the hyrax or rock-rabbit, whose urine, deposited in a layer on the rocks, may have entered into the composition of some of the pigments. Kaggen had an adopted daughter, Porcupine, who mated with Kwammanga, the rainbow. Their children were young Kwammanga and the Ichneumon. All these creatures had animal pets, a sign of the love of the Bushmen for animals, and an indication that, in spite of Francis Klingender's stigmatization of them as cruel and remorseless hunters, they really felt affection and compunction for the creatures that hunger compelled them to kill.

While it would probably not be true to say that the Triad of the ichneumon, porcupine, and rock rabbit never appear in the rock paintings — we have already noticed the brief appearance of a rock rabbit held in the hands of a giant hunter — it would be true to say that they play a very unimportant role in the paintings, both as regards the number of times that they appear and the parts that they play. How can this be if they were the mainstay of Bushman mythology? Supporters of the mythological theory would probably argue that either they are too sacred to be depicted at all, just as Christ was to the early Christians, or else they appear in the form of human beings, like werewolves who are undergoing the human phase of their two transformations. It is difficult to find them in the animal-headed men, simply because none of these men appear to have the heads of ichneumons or either of the other two basic mythological beasts.

The absence of the Triad also seems to dispose, as I have suggested elsewhere, of any need to find totemism as a source for the paintings. What remains? Many observers feel that the paintings are very much concerned with "rain animals," the mythological interpretation of the clouds that brought the rain. I would be the first to admit that rainmaking probably had a good deal to do with the creation of the

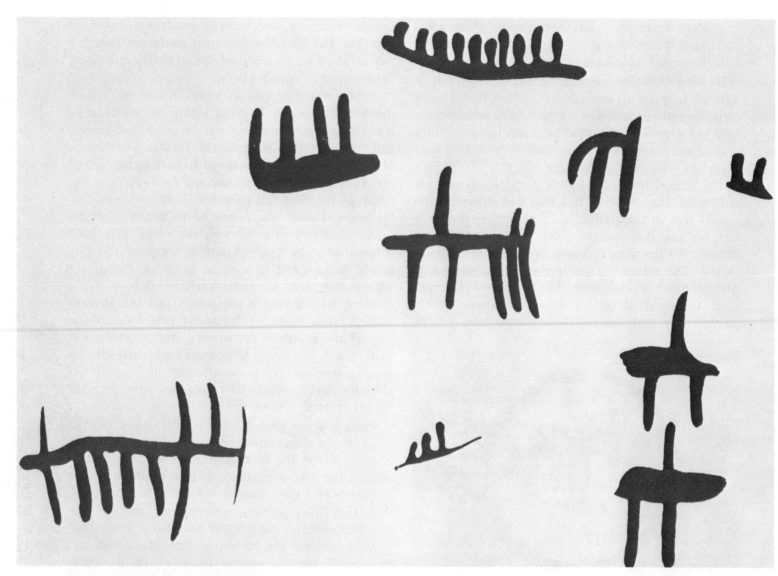

Stylized figures, which are probably conventionalized animals and humans in a canoe. (Painting by Helen Tongue. Photo by Stella Mayes Reed.)

paintings but I cannot wholeheartedly agree with all Alexander R. Willcox's identifications of strange-looking beasts, which emit streams of dashes from their mouths, as rain animals. To my mind they could equally well be hippopotamuses or other animals that have been badly drawn, and that have raised their head while drinking so that water streams from the corner of their muzzles.

The mythological interpretation of the paintings has been infused with new life by Francis Klingender, a writer of genius who was cut off before his due time. Klingender saw at the root of Bushman art a "ritual marriage and a ritual hunt."[2] He seized on the eight stories told to J. M. Orpen by a young Bushman

[2] Klingender, *Animals in Art and Thought,* p. 8.

named Qing, stories that were Qing's explanation of the paintings made by his own recently exterminated tribe in the Maluti Mountains.[3]

Kaggen was the chief protagonist in these tales. He fulfilled one of the primary purposes of any god in providing food for his worshippers. "Have you not hunted and heard his cry," Qing asked Orpen, "When the elands suddenly start and run to his call? Where he is, elands are in droves, like cattle."[4] Rather significantly, Qing added that he did not know what Kaggen was, which presumably meant that he would be unable to portray him. In fact we would no more expect to find a picture of Kaggen himself in the caves of the Bushmen than we would expect to find a portrayal of Jehovah in Solomon's temple — he was

[3] Ibid., p. 11.

[4] Ibid., p. 13.

148

unknowable, but his presence could be inferred from his associates, the elands.

Kaggen had created game, particularly elands, by leaving a little eland calf to grow up in a kloof, secluded and surrounded by hills and precipices. When Kaggen's sons interfered with the work of creation, spoiling it, he was at hand to correct their mistakes by showing them how to hunt the elands and to fabricate arrow poison. At the same time he punished his sons for their sin by killing them and afterwards bringing them to life. They were also inflicted with nose bleeding.

If it does nothing else, this myth emphasizes the sacredness of the caves and rock shelters — the stony womb of all created life; it also points to the existence of a deity whose presence is indicated by the gathering of game.

Klingender regarded the creations of the paintings as a rite of food magic. He was not content with this as the sole explanation of their existence, however; he felt that this was merely the superficial one, the only one that could be expressed outloud. He pointed out that Kaggen's sons had to observe certain rituals if their successes in the hunt were to continue, and he quotes one old Bushman who told Orpen that it was necessary to show respect for the game, otherwise they would go away. One way of showing respect for them, one suspects, was by painting their pictures on the walls of the rock shelters.

What about the rituals, taboos, and prohibitions that were laid on the Bushmen so that their supply of game should continue? Klingender, as I once commented in a review, was rarely content to take the beaten road of interpretation to any subject. Just as he suggested that the hunt of the wren, in medieval Europe, exemplified the desire of young knights and squires to murder their feudal lord and sleep with his lady, so he here insisted that these taboos are really

Another part of the same frieze. (Painting by Helen Tongue. Photo by Stella Mayes Reed.)

149

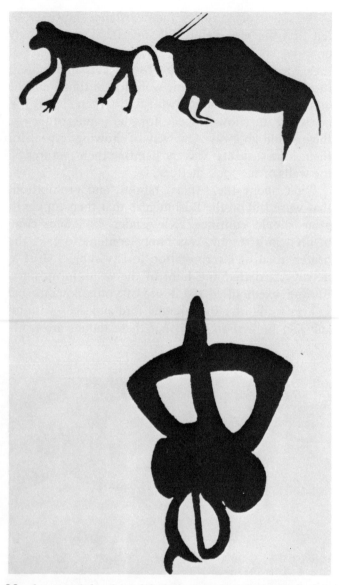

Monkey and buck, with below, a symbol. (Painting by Helen Tongue. Photo by Stella Mayes Reed.)

sexual taboos, not food taboos. They were in effect a prohibition against incest. The Bushmen would not have felt any guilt about killing animals which they had to expiate, Klingender suggests, because they liked hunting, so we must look for some deeper feeling of guilt.

Was Klingender right or wrong? It is impossible to tell but at least we can be agreed that the mythological interpretations of the paintings are inexhaustible. Just as the same picture suggests very different mythological interpretations to modern commentators, so we may be sure that it would suggest very different concepts to the Bushmen of old South Africa.

So far as I have been able to discover, there is one curious omission in the researches made into the paintings and their connection with folklore. No one, it would appear, ever asked the Bushmen a simple question such as, "Will these paintings secure good hunting for you?" Stow was probably so convinced that they were sympathetic magic paintings, that he never bothered to ask. The other observers may have omitted this question because they were afraid of frightening their informants. Magic is still a frightening subject in modern Africa today. Expatriate whites may joke about it readily enough on their first arrival on the continent, but as their experiences accumulate it becomes a matter, not for joking, but for grave concern.

Someone much nearer to the Bushmen than we will ever be, Dorothea Bleek, did not hesitate to scout completely the notion that the paintings were made for magical purposes. This she said would argue a foresight that was quite out of keeping with their nature.

"It is difficult to imagine one of these people, who live only for the hour and take no thought for the morrow, practising art till he had gained sufficient proficiency to make a picture that would be effective as a magical means of inspiring confidence in his fellow men. That would be absolutely out of keeping with the thoughtless, care-free cast of mind of the race. Whenever there is plenty and the sun shines they are happy; anxiety for the future never worries them."

The only possible explanation for the paintings, thought Miss Bleek, especially for the way that the rocks had been covered with superimposed pictures again and again, lay in the sheer love of art and a determination to make a better painting than those which already covered the rock face. It is very strange that this love of art for art's sake should have so completely deserted the modern Bushmen of the Kalahari, especially since art is a salable commodity. The modern Bantu in Rhodesia have been quick to turn to their profit the art centers provided by the government out of the taxes on African-style beer. Yet in the Kalahari though the Bushmen ornament tortoiseshells with beading, carve walking stick handles, and engrave ostrich eggshells, painting has disappeared.

Many observers have felt that the theories that have been enumerated so far are inadequate explanations of the paintings. They have suggested that the

Rhinoceros, ostrich, wildbeast, or gnu at Baviaan's Krantz. (Painting by Helen Tongue. Photo by Stella Mayes Reed.)

These deeply cut engravings from Zambia may represent animal spoor. For whatever reason, the ancient artists were fascinated by handprints, footmarks, and the spoor of animals. (Courtesy Zambian Tourist Board.)

schematic ones at least may be susceptible to a practical explanation. The symbols may represent ownership marks. These are used by many African people but they are usually much more elaborate than the symbols depicted in the paintings. These symbols, others say, are the recognition marks of secret societies. It is difficult to see why anything secret should be displayed openly on a cave wall, but as has been already noticed, there is a connection between the Dogon caves and the Mask Society and one Malawian cave and a *vinyau* society. Another explanation put forward is that the symbols expound an ethical code of conduct. We have already noticed that Mpunzi Hill in Malawi has a name that may be connected with initiation or teaching. Exhortations to the initiated painted on the wall have a long tradition in Africa. St. Augustine painted the Penitential Psalms on the wall of his bedroom in such large letters that he could read them even on his death bed. Much later Coptic hermits covered the walls of their caves with quotations from the Bible or the Fathers.

Other suggestions for the reasons for the paintings are that they were undertaken to while away an idle moment, or that some of them at least represent tallies, messages now indecipherable, that were left for friends or that they record memorable incidents. John Woolman, a Quaker of New Jersey in the eighteenth century, noticed at one of his camping places in the American wilderness figures of Indians that had been painted on the stripped trunks of trees, because the spot was "a path used heretofore by warriors." Similarly the rock paintings may be the chronicles of the land.

Any of the explanations that we have entertained hitherto could have some grain of plausibility about them, except for the one that is probably put forward most often, that the paintings were undertaken just for fun. There is nothing amusing about toiling up a hill, burdened by the equipment necessary for painting, as anyone who has ever copied an African rock painting may agree.

My own interpretation of the reason that the painters painted was suggested to me by an American lady whom I met briefly in the lounge of Nairobi airport. A devout churchwoman, she was returning from a tour of churches in a central African country, and in describing to me her experiences she mentioned that the Africans had a reverence for greatness, and particularly for great men. Small boys, she told me, would go and stand in the footsteps left by some

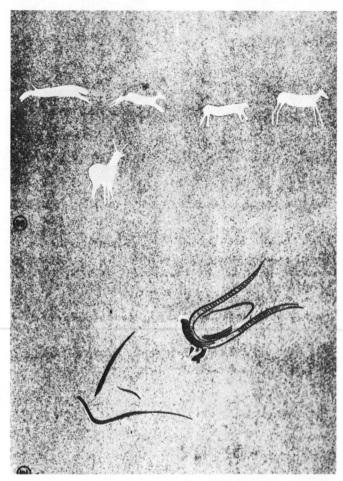

Leopards chasing rhebucks and birds. (Painting by Helen Tongue. Photo by Stella Mayes Reed.)

personage whom they admired and revered, pressing their feet into his tracks through the bush in the hope that some of the vestigial vital force that lingered in the footsteps would transfer itself to them. She described how she had seen some of the boys standing in the footsteps of their bishop. "Of course," she added "it becomes much less impressive when you learn that they go and stand in the tracks of automobiles as well."

The juxtaposition of the bishop and the automobile recalled to me suddenly that both of these subjects had been pictured in rock art, the bishop in the Congo in the sixteenth century, the automobile in Zambia in the twentieth.

What could be the connection between these apparently unrelated subjects and the kopjes, kloofs, mountains, rivers, running elands, charging rhinoceroses, the men and women locked in love or united by the joys of family life, neighbors meeting in counsel,

152

hunters confronting game, animals at bay, warriors in battle, and nations trekking? Some of the subjects must have seemed benign to the old hunters, others extremely malign. Why should the little people wish to represent old enemies like the rhinoceros and the crocodile, whose hide was impervious to their arrows, and new ones like the Bantu, the Boers, and the British soldiers?

There could be only one explanation. All these very diverse entities represented to the artists' eyes emanations of the vital force that upheld the universe.

To picture these objects was to transmit some at least of the vestigial force of their vitality. To behold them, better still to touch them, would convey some of that force into the person who came in contact with them. To place one's hand over an engraved handprint or a painted palm, to step into the footstep of Anna Xinga — or the much older hero for whose

Ostrich and giraffe at Roodekop. (Painting by Helen Tongue. Photo by Stella Mayes Reed.)

Dressed as a Matabele warrior, this Rhodesian guide points to a frieze of elands. (Photo Courtesy Rhodesian Ministry of Information.)

name hers had been substituted — to press one's finger against the fingermarks of the old artist who had made the dot and dash paintings by finger painting, to step on or touch the painted or engraved spoor, all this was to acquire the force of the persons or beings represented, as well as of the artists who had pictured them. To look at the rainbeast passing beneath the rainbow was to acquire the force of the thunder, to admire a battle scene was to acquire by osmosis the force of the warriors represented in it.

Hostile or not, the Boer trekkers affronting the wilderness, the Matabele impi clashing their spears on their shields as they advance, the British cavalry in their red coats, the Field Cornet riding in the midst of his commando, and directing their movements among a hail of poisoned arrows were as much a manifestation of that god that lived on high as the herds of elands in whose presence he manifested himself.

Stern realists whom the tenor of their life had

prevented from acquiring any illusions, the Bushmen and their earlier forebears recognized in their paintings the existence of a creator who had labored as much at creating the bad as well as the good. The poet William Blake had wondered whether the same God had made the tiger and the lamb. The rock artists knew that he had.

The whole purpose of rock painting was to mark the presence of the deity in certain favored spots, places that were "on high" like the god of the Hottentots, rock shelters and caves that personified the stony womb of creation. The subject of the paintings was relatively unimportant in that any painting, a single rhinoceros or a herd of elands, was a hymn to Creation, an acknowledgement of the power of that being who had created the starry heavens (figured perhaps in some of the symbols), the earth with its mountains and trees, animals, and men. The animals that as Kipling says, "being soulless are free from shame," appeared just as they were, painted realistically, but the men and women as if conscious of their unworthiness in appearing before their creator, are usually, though not always, disguised by their features being conventionalized or omitted. For the same motif, a medieval religious painter would paint sacred personages life size, but the donor of the picture would appear on a much reduced scale kneeling in a corner of the picture.

Had the Hottentots and Bushmen ever worshipped in the painted caves? Levaillant had collected the tradition that they did do this, and worship continued to be offered at specific caves all over Africa usually in connection with rainmaking. Probably the Bushmen and the Hottentots were the recipients of a religious tradition so old and transmitted so many times, from one civilization to another, that its tenets were but imperfectly understood though still devotedly carried out. In time, many of the messages of the cave paintings, though not all of them, had become abbreviated into symbols, a sort of religious shorthand that we can no longer decipher.

Persecution and extermination of the faithful do curtail the outward form of religious worship very considerably. Remnants of the Japanese Christians who survived the wholesale massacres of the seventeenth century continued to carry out religious rituals so truncated that they would bear little relationship to Christianity in the eye of the outside observer, but they were not addressed to him, but to God. Similarly, although we shall probably never unravel completely the symbolism of rock art (though we may receive some help in this direction if the Saharan script is ever deciphered), yet we can be reasonably sure of the purport, which had, as John Ruskin would have said, the same purpose as all art, to bring man nearer to God.

Index